D0192868

Also Available From the American Ac

Achieving a Healthy Weight for Your Child: An Action Plan for Families

ADHD: What Every Parent Needs to Know

Allergies and Asthma: What Every Parent Needs to Know

Autism Spectrum Disorders: What Every Parent Needs to Know

The Big Book of Symptoms: A–Z Guide to Your Child's Health

Building Resilience in Children and Teens: Giving Kids Roots and Wings

Caring for Your Adopted Child

Caring for Your School-Age Child: Ages 5 to 12

Caring for Your Teenager

CyberSafe: Protecting and Empowering Kids
in the Digital World of Texting, Gaming, and Social Media

Dad to Dad: Parenting Like a Pro

Food Fights: Winning the Nutritional Challenges of Parenthood
Armed With Insight, Humor, and a Bottle of Ketchup

Mama Doc Medicine: Finding Calm and Confidence in
Parenting, Child Health, and Work-Life Balance

Mental Health, Naturally: The Family Guide to Holistic Care
for a Healthy Mind and Body

My Child Is Sick! Expert Advice for Managing Common Illnesses and Injuries

Nutrition: What Every Parent Needs to Know

The Picky Eater Project: 6 Weeks to Happier, Healthier Family Mealtimes

Raising Kids to Thrive: Balancing Love With Expectations and Protection With Trust

Sleep: What Every Parent Needs to Know

Sports Success R$_x$! Your Child's Prescription for the Best Experience

Waking Up Dry: A Guide to Help Children Overcome Bedwetting

**For additional parenting resources, visit the HealthyChildren bookstore at
shop.aap.org/for-parents.**

 healthychildren.org
Powered by pediatricians. Trusted by parents.
from the American Academy of Pediatrics

Parenting Through Puberty

Mood Swings, Acne, and Growing Pains

Suanne Kowal-Connelly, MD, FAAP

American Academy of Pediatrics

DEDICATED TO THE HEALTH OF ALL CHILDREN®

American Academy of Pediatrics Publishing Staff

Mary Lou White, *Chief Product and Services Officer/SVP, Membership, Marketing, and Publishing*

Mark Grimes, *Vice President, Publishing*

Kathryn Sparks, *Manager, Consumer Publishing*

Shannan Martin, *Production Manager, Consumer Publications*

Linda Diamond, *Manager, Art Direction and Production*

Sara Hoerdeman, *Marketing Manager, Consumer Products*

Published by the American Academy of Pediatrics
345 Park Blvd
Itasca, IL 60143
Telephone: 630/626-6000
Facsimile: 847/434-8000
www.aap.org

The American Academy of Pediatrics is an organization of 67,000 primary care pediatricians, pediatric medical subspecialists, and pediatric surgical specialists dedicated to the health, safety, and well-being of infants, children, adolescents, and young adults.

The information contained in this publication should not be used as a substitute for the medical care and advice of your pediatrician. There may be variations in treatment that your pediatrician may recommend based on individual facts and circumstances.

Statements and opinions expressed are those of the author and not necessarily those of the American Academy of Pediatrics.

Products and Web sites are mentioned for informational purposes only and do not imply an endorsement by the American Academy of Pediatrics (AAP). The AAP is not responsible for the content of external resources. Information was current at the time of publication.

Brand names are furnished for identification purposes only. No endorsement of the manufacturers or products mentioned is implied.

The publishers have made every effort to trace the copyright holders for borrowed materials. If they have inadvertently overlooked any, they will be pleased to make the necessary arrangements at the first opportunity.

This publication has been developed by the American Academy of Pediatrics. The contributors are expert authorities in the field of pediatrics. No commercial involvement of any kind has been solicited or accepted in development of the content of this publication. Disclosures: The author reports no disclosures.

Every effort is made to keep *Parenting Through Puberty: Mood Swings, Acne, and Growing Pains* consistent with the most recent advice and information available from the American Academy of Pediatrics.

Special discounts are available for bulk purchases of this publication. E-mail our Special Sales Department at aapsales@aap.org for more information.

Printed in the United States of America
9-406   1 2 3 4 5 6 7 8 9 10
CB0107
ISBN: 978-1-61002-212-5
eBook: 978-1-61002-213-2
EPUB: 978-1-61002-220-0
Kindle: 978-1-61002-221-7
Cover design by Daniel Rembert
Book design by Linda Diamond
Library of Congress Control Number: 2017963219

What People Are Saying

Talking to kids about puberty is awkward and embarrassing for parents, but learning about the physical and emotional changes during puberty doesn't have to be. Dr Kowal-Connelly's book covers the current challenges facing our teenagers. This book is extremely well written and informative. I recommend this book to all parents and health care providers looking to equip themselves with the most up-to-date information about puberty.

Robert C. Lee, DO, MS, FAAP, associate pediatric program director, member of Bright Futures Expert Panel on Middle Childhood, NYU Winthrop Hospital

What a great resource! Dr Kowal-Connelly provides in-depth yet personal guidance on everything from why your teen should see her doctor one-on-one to the value of sports. Get a refreshing and valuable perspective along with hands-on advice about puberty, emotional changes, and all those unavoidable pitfalls of raising an adolescent.

Jack Levine, MD, FAAP, clinical assistant professor, Department of Pediatrics, Donald and Barbara Zucker School of Medicine at Hofstra/Northwell

This book is like having an "adolescence coach" to navigate you through the inevitable challenges of parenting through puberty! Dr Kowal-Connelly's nonjudgmental, beautifully positive tone makes the clinical relatable. She is clearly passionate about her work, and her devotion to young people and parenting shines through each section. Dr Kowal-Connelly "typicalizes" experiences of teens as well as parents who may have doubts about their own ability to understand and manage this journey. Filled with resources, checklists, and techniques to assist with important conversations, this book is very current, relevant, and empowering! Highly recommended!

Diana M. Filiano, DSW, director, child welfare training program, Stony Brook University School of Social Welfare

There is no better advocate, partner, role model, or mentor than a loving and willing parent. As a parent, we often feel hopelessly inadequate when met with the challenges of each stage of our child's development—the greatest and possibly the most dreaded being adolescence. While we all know there isn't a handbook for raising children successfully, it's nice to know we do have resources and this book is a must-have! While many of us remember this period of our own lives, the missing element is the insight or understanding of what was actually happening and why.

Parenting Through Puberty provides insights into the confusion, insecurities, frustration, and fears of many adolescents. This is a must read for all parents prior to or at any time during their child's adolescence. Turn to this book again and again as every child, at different stages of development, will present his or her own unique needs. This book is a way to provide a fresh perspective of your child's needs that may help provide parents with the tools to creatively navigate the ever-changing waters.

Sarah Collins-Molese, BSN, MA, SNT, lead nurse, Freeport Public Schools

Parenting Through Puberty is a must read for all parents of adolescents! Dr Suanne Kowal-Connelly provides realistic and practical suggestions to assist parents in navigating the tribulations that come along with raising children through puberty. Learn the nuts and bolts of what children go through, both physically and socially, as you raise healthy teens. As an educator for 25 years, I highly recommend this book!

Michelle Gallo, EdD, assistant superintendent, Baldwin School District

Parenting Through Puberty is thoughtfully crafted and wonderfully informative. Dr Kowal-Connelly provides parents with a resource that is easy to read, has accessible references for more information, and above all a positive approach to what can often seem a daunting period of child development. I would highly recommend this book to parents interested in supporting their child(ren) with confidence and affirmative strategies.

Joy Connolly, director of education program services, Child Care Council of Nassau, Inc.

Parenting Through Puberty provides parents with a map to successfully navigate through the rough road of parenting. Dr Kowal-Connelly identifies important checkpoints that help new and experienced parents along the way. This book outlines the natural phases of puberty and prepares parents to identify their child's puberty phase while predicting the physiological and behavioral reactions of children. As an educator, one of the biggest challenges for students is the coping with the changes in their body as they grow. *Parenting Through Puberty* offers parents information to successfully transition their child from childhood to young adulthood. As a parent of 3 children and an educator of 20+ years, I highly recommend this as a must read.

Eduardo Ramirez, director for physical education, health education, health services, and athletics, Baldwin Union Free School District

Dr Kowal-Connelly is a dedicated advocate for families. Her expert advice is conveyed through a lens of compassion and empathy.

Elizabeth Isakson, MD, FAAP, executive director, Docs for Tots

To my parents, Ted and Dorothy—

for the unconditional love they gave me;

my sister, Andrea—for her friendship;

my husband, Kenneth—for his infinite support;

and my sons, Daniel, Leland, and Adrian—

for fulfilling all my dreams of parenthood.

Contents

Acknowledgments

First and foremost, I want to thank my sister, Andrea E. Miller, for making me believe way back when that I had something worthwhile to say in a book. I also want to give a big shout-out to Amanda Krupa, MSc, the editor of HealthyChildren.org, because everything was set in motion the day that she welcomed me to become a contributor and later introduced me to Kathryn Sparks, the manager of consumer publishing at the American Academy of Pediatrics (AAP), who then went on to ask if I would like to publish with the AAP—a total dream come true! Thank you, Kathryn. You have been my rock through this entire process and despite its challenges, I simply loved working together.

I also want to voice my appreciation for the input of many pediatric colleagues and AAP staff for reviewing and offering their suggestions on the manuscript.

Sarah Armstrong, MD, FAAP

Jonathan Fanburg, MD, FAAP

Meredith Loveless, MD, FAAP

Paul Stricker, MD, FAAP

Yovanni Young Millings

Beth Westbrook Starnes

I appreciate and value Lucy Weinstein, MD, FAAP, and Dina Joy Lieser, MD, FAAP, for their peer review of the manuscript and recognize the time they took out of their busy lives to do so.

I am so grateful to Dr Tyrone Howell, whose mentoring made it easy for me to excel in so many areas that were entirely foreign to me, like Web site development, blog writing, and having a social media presence, all of which prepared me to have success as an author.

I wish that my father was here to read this, as he sadly passed away while I was writing the book. He was my greatest cheerleader and unwavering in his support of my aspirations and dreams of becoming a physician. Although, growing up, I found my mother's approach to be much less inspiring (and much less fun than my dad's), she was the one who jumped in the trenches with me and unceremoniously red-marked projects, compositions, and term papers until they were successfully completed with excellence. I eventually learned to appreciate the value of both their styles and treasure their influences on my life.

To my husband, Kenneth Connelly, I say thank you, and thank you again for your infinite support and love. My life changed forever the day that I met you. To my boys, Daniel, Leland, and Adrian—nothing could ever inspire me more than the joy and love that I felt the day that each of you were born, and you continue to be the lights in my life always.

And finally, it is truly the hundreds of families that I have cared for who have made this all possible. You have all touched my life and continue to touch my life in extraordinary ways. I thank each and every one of you, even those who might have preferred my older and wiser partners, the late Dr Leonard F. Rosenzweig, Dr Bernard P. Leonard, and Dr Andrew L. Ageloff, for continuing to enlighten and teach me every day.

Introduction

Everything we do has purpose. The key is *to see that purpose* and do something with it. After nearly 30 years in private practice, I am now a pediatrician who works for a health system dedicated to caring for the underserved communities on Long Island. I have been a school physician for several local districts, as well as a New York State trainer for child abuse and neglect. Finally, I am a dedicated triathlete. The dots that make up my life seem to fit together into a firm conviction that everything I do today services some purpose in improving the well-being of families and their children.

My Web site, Health Powered By You, LLC, is where I post information about child health, family dynamics, and wellness-related topics. I contribute articles to HealthyChildren, and now I have had the opportunity to write this book! I embrace this incredible opportunity to share my stories and expertise in an effort to make the adolescent experience less mysterious and more successful for parents.

Welcome to Puberty (Again!)

No doubt you have heard more than your fair share of information on this stage of life. This wonderful and magical period is when your child's evolution into adulthood begins. Before your eyes is the metamorphosis of your child's body and mind into a young adult. At no time since the first year of life has anything happened this rapidly. It is the gateway to the wondrous world ahead.

So why then is this period fraught with such ambivalence? Why do we as parents, and sometimes as pediatricians, not choose words, such as *magical,* to describe the anticipation of adolescence and puberty? I think a big stumbling block is that puberty and adolescence are a complex and somewhat chaotic time.

One element that adds to the complexity of this period is the indisputable pace at which physical growth and thinking patterns are changing. It is difficult to grasp the enormity of the multitude of marvelous though nuanced changes that are taking place. The last time you had to deal with so much rebelliousness was around the age of two. However, it is so much cuter to deal with 2-year-olds stamping their feet and demanding their independence than it is with 14-year-olds. Yet this stage is no less magical and, in many ways, more profound. I aim to help you parent through puberty with less fear and more joy.

My strategy is very simple. By sharing meaningful information, evidence-based knowledge, and anecdotal experiences relevant to topics that have come up regularly within my practice, teaching, and school health career, I hope you have a more comprehensive perspective of puberty and the adolescent issues that are present, making it easier to feel more secure and confident.

In This Book

The first chapter of this book covers the nuts and bolts of what happens to children's bodies as they go through puberty. The second chapter deals with the major issues of self-esteem and body image, which affect many adolescents. Particularly, I focus on how body image is affected by media messages. In Chapter 3, I address concerns that many parents have regarding the timing of puberty—some worry it is early and some worry that it is late! I also discuss performance-enhancing substances that are often taken by teens who are impatient for their bodies to become larger, faster, and stronger.

In Chapter 4 you will discover that the developing brain of your teenager really *is* different! And in Chapter 5, I describe how to tell the difference between teenage moodiness and depression. I also cover some methods that can help your teen manage the anxiety that can be present while working through puberty.

Chapter 6 solves the mystery of what pediatricians talk about to your teen behind closed doors and offers insight into why this one-on-one visit is very important! Chapter 7 begins the portion of the book that provides guidance on raising healthy teens in healthy families. It talks about maintaining a healthy weight and pursuing physical activities.

Chapter 8 provides guidance for navigating puberty with children with special needs. Chapter 9 introduces you to the topic of physical literacy (yes, it's just as important as reading literacy!) while Chapter 10 describes how to makes changes in your family that will improve everyone's health and wellness. Adolescence is the time that many habits are set, and it is critical to your teen's future health to establish smart routines now that will last a lifetime.

More than any other emotion, parents tell me that adolescence *worries* them. Admittedly, it worried me too when my sons and stepdaughter were teens. But I have long believed that the more anticipatory guidance parents have, the more prepared we are to handle the challenges that arise.

There is no right or defined way to parent. But when parents are well versed with evidence-based facts, professional advice, examples, and insight into the teenage mindset, your parenting beliefs and decisions can come from a more confident place of love and wisdom.

A career in pediatrics has been my lifelong dream come true. *Parenting Through Puberty* is the culmination of a lifetime's labor of great joy and love that I hope will enlighten parents and teens alike.

PART

The Physical Changes

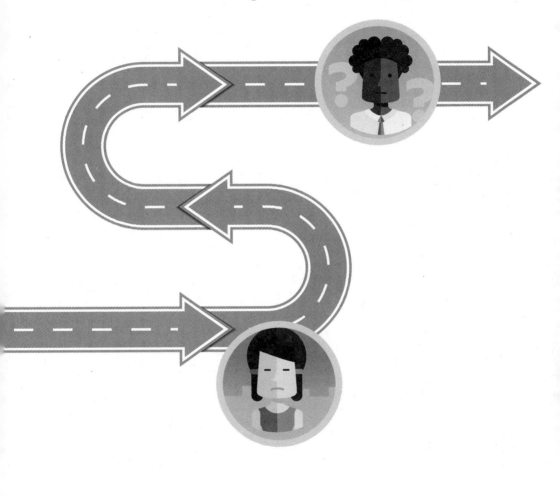

CHAPTER 1

The Basics of Physical Growth During Puberty

Parents who wish to do more than simply survive their child's puberty and adolescence need to understand the physical and emotional stages of this exceptional time. The more you know about puberty and the changes it brings, the better able you are to help your adolescent through this challenging phase and to support him or her as he or she moves through adolescence. You will have fewer surprises and bumps along the way when you know all the variations of normal development.

You may feel that you understand adolescence because, after all, you went through it! But just because we drive a car doesn't mean we understand how the engine works! Further, many families consist of single parents or same-sex parents. Parents may need to have critical conversations with children of the opposite sex, with no partner of the opposite sex to provide perspective. There is no reason that Dad can't matter-of-factly discuss his daughter's changes as well as Mom can, and vice versa. The more all parents understand what is happening on a physical and emotional level, the better they can care for their children in a way that makes a difference.

This Can't Be Happening Already!

Let's tackle the physical aspects of puberty first. As a parent, the way you matter-of-factly deal with the changes your child is experiencing will help your child feel less uncertain and more confident about him- or herself. One way to be matter-of-fact is to use appropriate language and terminology when speaking about the body and its changes. Using another word or version of your child's body parts and their physical changes may give your child the impression that it is wrong to use the appropriate terminology, when it is actually very much appropriate and is nothing to be ashamed or embarrassed about.

Doctors divide puberty into different stages called Tanner stages or sexual maturity ratings. However, the system we will use in this book divides puberty into 5 different stages, puberty stages (PS) 1 to 5. Everyone starts out at puberty stage 1. A child in puberty stage 1 has not yet entered puberty.

Let's Begin With the Girls

By the time most parents realize that their daughter has entered puberty, it has often been around for a few months, possibly a little longer. Girls often will have an increase in fat just before any changes occur. This is the body's way of readying for change.

Puberty Stage

The Budding Begins

The weight gain that occurs before puberty often goes unnoticed. The very first significant sign of puberty is *breast budding,* and this means that a girl has entered puberty stage 2. Often, only the girl may be aware of this. Breast budding typically begins between ages 8 and 13 years, and refers to the growth of a smooth, round, firm, and rubbery nodule underneath the nipple and areola. The bud is usually about the size of a pea. More often than not, it begins on only one side, and many girls may not mention it. Sometimes the breast bud is very tender when it is bumped.

Often, changes in a girl's behavior are because of difficulties with accepting and feeling comfortable about her changing body. You may recognize this behavior and be able to offer support. Remember that, with a short visit, your child's pediatrician also is ready to help relieve your daughter's fears about puberty.

When girls enter puberty before age 8 years, it is considered early, and after age 13 years it is considered late. If this is the situation with your daughter, speak with your daughter's pediatrician about why this might be and what, if anything, should be done. Often nothing is necessary, and your daughter's development is simply a variation of healthy growth. We will discuss more on this topic in Chapter 3.

Some girls become very anxious and self-conscious when the breasts begin to grow, and they begin to shy away from activities that they previously loved, such as dancing or playing sports. Knowing that this can happen can help parents discuss and provide reassurance and support.

A Quick Guide to Breast Development

- Breast budding is the first sign of puberty for girls.
- Early on, bumping into the breast bud can be quite painful!
- After budding, the breast will begin to grow into a small mound.
- One breast usually develops at a time.
- The breasts can develop and remain uneven for a few years.
- Breast sizes usually even out, but breasts are never exactly symmetrical.

When Do Parents Consider Having the "Period Talk"?

After breast budding, parents may wonder if this is a good time to have that "special talk" to prepare their daughter for her period. After breast budding, most girls will have approximately 2 years before their period arrives, though some will have less. Girls, particularly those who are between 8 and 10 years old at this stage, just need the minimum degree of information to be comfortable. A parent may simply say that this is just the very, very early beginning of breasts. If your daughter is older than 10 or 11 and her friends have already begun menstruating, or she wishes to know more and seems receptive, it is important that

you establish yourself as willing and able to talk about her changing body. This way she will come to you with questions when they arise.

The first menstrual cycle usually begins about 2 years after the breast buds appear.
The appearance of breast buds might not be the right time for the "period talk," but is a good time to discuss her changing body.

Many girls at this stage have not yet had the classic fifth-grade health class yet, do not know what menstruation is, do not want to think about it at all, and are not emotionally ready to learn about it. If you insist on having "the period talk" to a girl not yet ready for it, you may find yourself lecturing on the subject with your child's hands covering her ears, chanting nonsense loudly to drown out your words.

During puberty stage 2, girls will begin to grow a few, slightly pigmented, straight hair on the part of the labia where the labial lips meet. The labia are the thick, cushiony outside part of the vagina. The appearance of pubic hair in puberty stage 2 usually begins about 3 months after breast budding. At this time, you might notice a body odor and you should talk to your daughter about using deodorant and taking regular showers or baths.

You may be anxious about the arrival of menstruation (dreading the irritability that may come along with it), or you may delight in the changes that are clearly starting. Your daughter's period is still nearly 2 years away, so it is not yet time to create a little care package for her to carry around, just in case.

The growth of pubic hair is another time that might make you think that menstruation will begin soon. However, the start of the menstrual cycle is not associated with the hormones that cause the growth of pubic hair. Breast budding usually precedes pubic hair by approximately 3 months, so the period will usually still be about 21 months away for 70% of girls.

Puberty Stage

3

The Mound Begins

In puberty phase 3, the breast and areola, which is the darker area around the nipple, enlarge but appear as all one unit without any contour separation. The breast becomes a small mound that protrudes from the chest. At this point, one of two things tends to happen. Parents who want to celebrate this new development in the best way they know how may take their daughter to the mall to pick up a bra or two. Other parents (who also wish to celebrate this stage) may have daughters who want to forget that all of these changes are occurring. Girls who resist celebrating puberty are more often than not early bloomers and, like most kids, they don't want to be different. If their best friend isn't growing breasts, then they don't want them either. It may be helpful to speak frankly to your daughter about the changes she is going through. The more positive you can be, the more you help your daughter to respond positively.

Addressing Changes

Parents can help their daughter feel more comfortable with her changing body by letting her know everyone eventually goes through it. Ask her if she has any questions you can help answer. Take her to the bookstore and let her pick out a book that explains how her changing body develops as she ages. Go shopping with her to buy her first bra. Once she gets her period, create a cute care package with necessary supplies, such as tampons, pads, or underwear liners, that she can place in her bag while at school for when she does need to use it.

Comfort her and if she has any questions she feels uncomfortable about, reassure her that you are there for her, but that she can also address her concerns with any female family member, school nurse, or her pediatrician.

In puberty stage 3, the pubic hair is now darker and starting to curl, and the amount has increased. The hair is confined to the top of the labia and does not extend to the thighs. Earlier, it may not have appeared like much, but it is now quite noticeable.

- Girls' growth spurt usually will begin between puberty stage 2 and puberty stage 3.

- Growth begins with the enlargement of the feet and hands, followed next by arms and legs, and finally by the trunk and chest.

- The growth spurt has begun when a girl's shoe size appears to change overnight from a child's size to an adult's size.

- During the growth spurt, armpit hair (also called axillary hair) may begin to grow.

- A clear or thin, white vaginal discharge may begin, and although parents sometimes get very nervous about this, there is no need to be.

- Acne (also referred to as pimples or zits) may begin to form. (For more information, see Zeroing In on Acne text box)

The growth spurt usually begins to accelerate within 6 months of breast budding. Approximately 30% of girls in puberty stage 3 will start having their period now, which is earlier than most girls, who begin it in puberty stage 4.

The gawky tween stage occurs because the typical pattern is growth of the outer part of the body (hands and feet, then legs and arms) before the trunk grows. When parents comment that their daughter or son is all arms and legs, it is literally true for a while!

Puberty Stage

She's Looking Like a Grown-up

During puberty stage 4, the areola and developing nipple form a secondary mound that distinguishes itself from the surrounding breast tissue. In this stage, the breast begins to fill out and become adultlike. Time to go back to the mall for some new clothes!

During puberty stage 4, pubic hair is coarser and curly, and there is more of it. But there is still less than in an adult, and it does not spread to the thighs. The pubic hair has not finished developing, but there is now a distinct triangle of hair, whereas in previous stages it was not as well-defined.

For most girls, growth will peak approximately 1 year after it starts. The typical growth of 2 to 2½ inches per year will approach 4 inches in one year during this time. Most girls' periods will start in puberty stage 4, often approximately 6 months after peak height velocity has been reached.

Getting taller comes before weight increases. So, filling out comes later by several months. Muscle mass increases and strength follows. A difficult issue for many girls to accept about their bodies is the additional weight gain. In prepubertal boys and girls, lean muscle mass is approximately 80%, but it will decrease to 75% in girls as subcutaneous fat begins to accumulate.

Zeroing In on Acne

Acne is a dreaded feature of puberty that affects more than 80% of teenagers. Teens often feel they need to clean their skin better or eat differently to have healthier skin. In reality, acne is not a result of poor hygiene or due to food.

Acne is caused by changes to hormone levels that result in an increased and thicker production of an oily secretion called sebum. Sebum lubricates the skin and protects it, but during puberty it has a tendency to clump together with dead skin cells and other debris, blocking skin pores, causing them to become infected or inflamed. This results in different forms of acne that protrude as whiteheads, blackheads, pustules, nodules, or cysts.

Acne often runs in families. The majority of cases are mild and will heal without scarring. For the prevention of minor blemishes and mild to moderate acne, over-the-counter lotions containing benzoyl peroxide can be helpful. Your pediatrician or a dermatologist will be able to prescribe treatment for more severe or persistent acne. Sometimes acne in girls may be the result of an underlying hormonal imbalance with the overproduction of the male hormone testosterone, which is part of a condition called polycystic ovarian syndrome (PCOS) and can be treated.

Teenagers should be aware that oily creams and lotions can block skin follicles and enhance the buildup of sebum. These skin and hair products should be avoided. It is better to use unscented, water-based products.

Puberty Stage

All Grown Up

In puberty stage 5, the nipple will project from the areola, which is now part of the general mature breast tissue. Like it or not, breast development is now complete. Change can be new and scary, but sometimes what seems like a bad thing is perfect once it is given a chance. Do your best to encourage your daughter to love her body exactly the way it is.

In puberty stage 5 there is an adult feminine triangle of hair spreading to the surface of the thighs. Most teens would prefer to have the pubic hair development stop at puberty stage 4, but, alas, we don't get to control such matters. Pubic hair growth that reaches the thighs marks the end of puberty.

In this stage, linear growth slows and, in general, most girls will grow taller for no more than 2 years after the start of their period. Their height will increase by no more than 2 inches following the start of their period, and on average, most girls will only gain ½ to 1 inch more in height. Adult height in girls is usually reached by 16 years. Most girls will gain a total of approximately 25 pounds by the end of puberty.

For a complete summary of the 5 puberty stages for girls, see Table 1-1.

A Quick Recap of the Main Physical Events of Puberty in Girls

- Breast budding begins, followed by the menstrual cycle approximately 2 years later for 70% of girls (and earlier for the rest).
- Before the girl's period begins, the following steps occur:
  - Approximately 6 months after the breast budding, shoe size increases quickly.
  - About 6 months after the shoe size change, height begins to skyrocket, which is called peak height velocity. It usually occurs in puberty stages 2 and 3.
  - The girl's period begins about 6 months from the time of peak height velocity.
- In the later stages of puberty, a small amount of growth is still possible, but usually growth is about ½ or 1 inch and does not exceed 2 inches. Height does not increase beyond 2 years from the beginning of a girl's period.

On to the Boys

Puberty Stage

Just Getting Started

With boys, things generally happen a little differently than with girls. One of the biggest differences is that most boys are more excited about the prospects of having their body parts change. They can't develop fast enough. Bigger genitalia, more body hair, large muscles—these are the things worth celebrating!

Boys typically experience an increase in fat tissue before they enter puberty stage 2. At this stage, the testicles start to enlarge slightly and become somewhat pink and less smooth. Next, there is slight enlargement of the penis, and finally, some pubic hair will begin to develop. It will be sparse, long, and slightly pigmented.

Enlargement of Testicles and Erections

The very first sign of puberty is enlargement of the testicles and their sac, the scrotum. This can begin as early as age 9 years to as late as age 14 years. There is a very wide variation in development that is entirely healthy for boys. There is more on this in Chapter 3. A child who does not fit within the range of typical development can be evaluated by a pediatrician; sometimes, a pediatric endocrinologist will be asked to assist in identifying any possible problem.

Penile erections start to become a more frequent occurrence because of male sex hormonal stimulation. Penile erections are normal in boys and can occur from the youngest of ages, even before birth! All boys experience erections when they don't anticipate them; they often occur during sleep. Boys will have done nothing to cause erections, and they can be

a huge source of embarrassment for boys. However, they can't do anything about this sometimes unwelcome event; it is simply a part of getting older.

Talk with your son about managing socially awkward penile erections. Suggest that he untuck his shirt or buy him tighter underwear instead of baggy boxer shorts. Your son might carry a folder at school to hold in front of himself when necessary. Above all, let him know it is entirely typical.

Puberty Stage

3

Adding Some Volume

During puberty stage 3, the pubic hair is darker and begins to curl, but it is still only a small amount. The penis becomes longer, and there may be a small amount of widening; the testes are still enlarging but are not adult size.

A boy's highest growth period begins between puberty stage 3 and puberty stage 4 with gains in height of usually about 4 inches in just the first year. Most of the increased fat tissue from the prepubertal period is lost during this growth spurt. With rapid growth and the loss of fat, some boys appear thin to parents. Once the growth spurt is completed, the weight will return.

Breast Tissue Growth

Breast budding and some enlargement of breast tissue will develop in approximately 40% to 65% of boys. This is called *gynecomastia,* and, as with girls, bumping into the breast can cause short-lived exquisite pain. Gynecomastia can be a source of extreme anxiety and embarrassment for boys; however, less than 10% of boys have enough enlargement that it causes excessive embarrassment or anxiety. Reassure your son that this will not be permanent and that it will go away within 3 years in 90% of boys. Only very rarely does gynecomastia require any treatment.

Puberty stage 3 marks the beginning of your son eating you out of house and home!

Voice Cracking

Puberty stage 3 is the most typical period for the embarrassing, often dreaded, cliché of adolescent boyhood—voice cracking. Voice cracking is due to growth in the larynx (voice box) and the vocal cords themselves, which are stretching to their new size. Although it varies for each boy, typically voice cracking will disappear by age 17 or 18 when the vocal cords have finished growing.

During this stage, one recurring question that boys have about their specific development is—"When will I start to grow taller?" Boys have discovered that they are maturing, and they start to sit up and take notice. They want to know when they are going to get taller, and they want to know how much taller they will get. It is, of course, exceptionally difficult to predict height exactly, and although I tend not to offer this because it is not always consistent with everyone, other doctors may use this formula:

During puberty stages 3 and 4, boys' dreams begin to take on a sexual nature and, for many boys, penile emissions begin. These penile emissions of semen occur during the night while sleeping and are typical during puberty. These are also referred to as "wet dreams." Some boys have a lot of wet dreams and some have a few or none at all. Everything is typical.

- Add the mother's height and the father's height in inches.

- Add 5 inches (for girls you would subtract 5 inches)

- Divide by 2.

Puberty Stage

4

Triangle Formation

In puberty stage 4, boys' pubic hair is now adultlike, but it does not extend to the thighs. Although it has not finished developing, there is now a distinct triangle of hair, whereas in previous stages it was not as well defined. The penis continues to enlarge, and its breadth increases to nearly adult size. The scrotum becomes larger and darker.

During puberty stage 4, boys may still experience rapid growth. Boys generally enter puberty later than girls, and this rapid growth occurs approximately 2 years after their genitals enlarge, usually between puberty stage 3 and puberty stage 4. This is why girls are so much taller than boys at the same age.

During this stage, your son's hair should begin to appear on his extremities, armpits, and his upper lip. If voice cracking and gynecomastia didn't already occur in puberty stage 3, they might occur in this stage. Pimples typically begin forming in this stage.

Toward the later part of puberty stage 4, boys typically begin to put weight back on, most of it as muscle. Their strength increases, and they appear filled out. In boys, fat composition decreases and muscle mass increases to 90%.

Before puberty stage 4, a young boy's physiology does not support muscle growth or development. Trying to make that happen when the body is not ready is like a frail 85-year-old person deadlifting to build physique. There are safe methods to support your son's fitness at all stages of puberty, and those methods should not exceed the current developmental stage of your child. Before puberty stage 4, children (boys and girls) cannot yet support muscle enhancement and attempts at heavy weight training and bodybuilding can result in serious injury.

Now, and not before this time, as boys have reached the full stage of puberty stage 4, the addition of weight and muscle make it safe to engage in reasonable heavy weight training.

Puberty Stage

All Grown Up

In puberty stage 5, the pattern of pubic hair is adultlike and spreads to the inner thighs. The penis and testes have reached adult size. By the end of puberty, boys will have gained, on average, 40 pounds (much of it muscle) and approximately 8 inches in height. A boy's adult height is usually reached by age 18 years.

A Quick Recap of the Main Physical Events of Puberty in Boys

- At first, the testicles increase slightly in size and the penis becomes somewhat elongated.
- About 3 months later, a slight amount of pubic hair appears.
- Approximately 2 years later, the growth spurt is in full bloom.
- The start of the growth spurt can be recognized by the rapid change in shoe size to an adult size.
- With the growth spurt comes growth in the vocal cords and the onset of voice cracking.
- The genitals continue to mature, and body hair growth, voice deepening, pimple formation, and other changes continue.
- Once the most rapid period of growth is finished, adding weight begins (made up mostly of muscle).

For a complete summary of the 5 puberty stages for boys, see Table 1-1.

Table 1-1. Summary of Puberty Stages and Development for Boys and Girls

Puberty Stage	Starting Age Range & Progression of Changes	Boys	Starting Age Range & Progression of Changes	Girls
1	Prepuberty	Puberty has not begun, but an increase in weight occurs.	Prepuberty	Puberty has not begun, but some increase in weight takes place.
2	9–14 years	The testes and scrotum begin to enlarge.	8–13 years	Breast budding begins.
		The first pubic hairs might appear.		The first pubic hairs appear.
		A slight amount of enlargement to the penis might occur.		Body odor is evident.
		Body odor is evident.		The first signs of the growth spurt appear (hands and feet enlarge).
				Some additional increase in weight might occur.
3	Within 2 years after PS 2 has begun	The penis definitely becomes enlarged, more in length than in width.	Approximately 3–6 months after PS 2 has begun	The breasts enlarge.
		Definite pubic hair appears.		The pubic hair begins to curl.
		The testes and scrotum continue to enlarge.		Menstruation may begin.
		The first signs of the growth spurt may appear (hands and feet enlarge).		The growth spurt is in full swing.
		Possible gynecomastia occurs.		Axillary hair grows.
		Voice cracking is possible.		Some vaginal discharge may begin.
		Wet dreams begin.		Pimples may appear.

Table 1-1. Summary of Puberty Stages and Development for Boys and Girls (continued)

Puberty Stage	Starting Age Range & Progression of Changes	Boys	Starting Age Range & Progression of Changes	Girls
④	Approximately 3 years after PS 2 has begun	The testes and scrotum continue to enlarge, with darkening. The penis grows, especially in width.	Approximately 2 years after PS 2 has begun	The breasts have more volume, and the nipples are distinct.
		The pubic hair is adultlike, but distribution of hair is not.		Menstruation occurs most commonly now.
		Gynecomastia is more common now.		The pubic hair is adultlike, but distribution of hair is not.
		Axillary hair begins, maybe some facial hair.		
		The growth spurt is in full swing.		
		Pimples may appear.		
⑤	Approximately 4 years after PS 2 has begun	The male is considered mature.	Approximately 4 years after PS 2 has begun	The female is considered mature.
		Growth is slowed and ends. For a very small percentage, the peak of growth is now.		Growth is slowed and ends.
		The pubic hair extends to inner thighs.		The pubic hair extends to inner thighs.
		Muscles are developing and growing.		In a very small percentage, menstruation occurs now.

Puberty Is a Process

Puberty is truly one of the most fascinating aspects of human development. During the time that children are growing, especially through puberty, parents become curious about how things are going to change, how much time it will take, and what they can expect. Girls and boys in early puberty advance in a similar manner from the prepubertal period of puberty stage 1 to puberty stage 2.

Given the uniqueness of every individual, some predictions are tougher to make than others, but the stages of puberty are not great mysteries. We are so much more alike than we might realize. The most profound truth about all people is not how unique they are, but how alike they are despite their uniqueness. There is a pattern to growth, and once the human body begins the process of puberty, within a designated range of time, development progresses in a predictable fashion.

Body Image Is Everything

There isn't a parent around who looks at his or her child and doesn't see something beautiful. Yes, our kids think that we just say they are beautiful because we're their parents. To some degree it's true, but to a large extent it's not. Children are so beautiful! There is something magnificent about youth; their innocence radiates all around them, from inside and out, from the way that they move to the way that they simply live life. We see it and we feel it, and even though there is no way to make them believe it, you know it's the truth!

> Did you know that 42% of first- through third-grade girls are dissatisfied with their looks and want to be thinner? It is quite typical for girls to have extra weight by the third grade and compare themselves to adult standards. As a parent, help explain to your daughter the changes her body is going through and will continue to go through, so she understands the puberty process.

What makes your child look in the mirror and not see what you see? As your children approach and go through puberty, with its multitude of physiologic and psychological changes, it can be difficult for them and for parents to adjust and accept what is happening. For some, not being satisfied with their looks has already occurred, even before puberty. Puberty may simply exacerbate a problem that already exists. For many tweens and teens, the problems surrounding body image are rooted in poor self-esteem. Self-esteem is the self-perception that a child has, the value the child perceives others see in him or her, and the child's attitude toward his or her own self-worth.

Promoting Self-esteem

Self-esteem is not in our DNA. It develops from our innate perceptions and from the way we interpret experiences in our lives. Self-esteem particularly depends on the way a child interprets the interactions of relatives and friends. How is your child seen and valued in your family? How do you and your significant other treat him or her as compared to others in the household? What are your expectations for your child? How do others who are highly valued by your child—siblings, friends, teachers, and relatives—interact with him or her? The more that your child believes that expectations have been achieved and satisfied, the better your child's self-esteem will be.

All children are different, and, thus, they handle personal issues in their own ways. Every parent sees this firsthand and has shared countless conversations with me about how astonishing it is to have raised siblings in the same house, with the same parents, and yet have them emerge with such unique and different personalities.

Even with the range of personalities that exist, there are things that parents can do to help foster a strong sense of self and combat the pervasive discontent in body image that you so often see in the tweens and teens that you love.

Help Your Child Develop a Sense of Security

Children need to feel secure about themselves and their future to effectively set and pursue their goals. Spend time talking with your child about things that you may take for granted, such as the fact that the images we see in magazines, movies, on TV, or on the Internet are not the norm. Try to discuss how extreme these images are and that they are not the only way to define beauty. Be careful not to be critical of weight issues, as weight shaming has been shown to not help with motivating weight control and can have the opposite effect. Rather than discussing the need to lose weight, it is much more useful to stress the value of a healthy active lifestyle. Parents should talk regularly with their children and encourage them to pursue areas in which they excel. Find possibly overlooked areas to point out your child's strengths. You should be your child's loudest cheerleader.

Help Your Child Have a Sense of Belonging

Providing a sense of belonging and making sure your child knows that he or she is valued and loved builds the foundation for a confident adolescent. This starts in the home, and when it is successful, the effect can foster even deeper relationships with family, friends, and school. Without this sense of acceptance, your child may feel rejected and isolated. Everyone needs to feel as part of a home, family, or group. Look for ways to admire your family's place in the world. Find the positive aspects that make up your family unit. Your family may consist of just you and your daughter or son, but that doesn't prevent your ability to instill a great sense of belonging and pride in your child. Families big and small can teach and model the value of volunteering together at their community center. In a family of any size, a teen can be asked to contribute to the household by giving him or her tasks that he or she alone is responsible for. Encourage your child to help out during after-school programs, such as a student mentoring program, or join a club or sport that is fun, such as theater or soccer. All of these activities foster a sense of belonging and a sense of responsibility, accomplishment, and pride, fostering great self-esteem.

Specific Ways to Help Children Develop Self-esteem

Why am I here? Eventually, we all ask ourselves this question, and, not uncommonly, we ask it for the first time during adolescence. Successful adulthood is built on setting goals, making plans for achieving those goals, and executing those plans. These years are the time to help your children explore and discover their passions, encourage them to follow their dreams, and help them express themselves well. Nurture your children in this manner, rather than urging a specific direction your child should take. It is important for your child to be in a field that he or she enjoys.

You might ask older teens about their goals for school and their lives. Some adolescents might have well-defined goals early on, while others are unsure. For adolescents who have a clear idea of goals, commend them on having direction, but caution them to be open-minded about new ideas that may come their way.

Do not be concerned about those teens without a plan. Being young is the time to develop a sense of who they are and what they like, to allow themselves time to explore their interests, and to follow their hearts. Developing goals and a purpose is much more about being true to oneself than it is about making concrete decisions.

It might be helpful for kids without direction to volunteer in different fields. Check for volunteer opportunities through their school and your community. Even a quick online search can provide many opportunities to get involved.

Help Your Child Feel Personal Competence and Pride

The goal of successful parenting is to raise competent, happy, healthy, independent adults. To achieve this, your child must have a sense of confidence that comes from taking chances and having personal rewarded successes, independent of parental efforts. Children must believe that they can stand and even jump and land on their own 2 feet. Finding that balance of being available, while not overshadowing and overpowering their initiative and independence, is key to their empowerment.

Help Your Child Have a Sense of Trust

To build a sense of trust in your child, you must model trustworthy behavior. "Do as I say and not as I do" won't cut it! If you want your child to be reliable and prompt, you must be that person too. If you want your child to adhere to rules such as no texting while driving and no phones or TV during meals, you must model this behavior. Once you have properly set the stage, trust that you have done your job well and put your faith in your child.

Help Your Child Have a Sense of Responsibility

If you know that your child is ready, give him or her the wheel, figuratively and literally. This is probably one of the hardest tasks for parents, but there is strength in numbers. All parents know how this feels. Remember how it made you feel when you were handed the keys to the family car. There's no feeling like it!

Younger adolescents may often ask to go to the mall alone with friends. You may have a million reasons why you don't want to allow this. However, most of those reasons may have nothing to do with your children and everything to do with their friends and issues outside of your children's control. If you trust your children, and you trust their friends, allow them the independence. With that independence comes responsibility, which often builds self-esteem. There may be bumps along the road toward independence, but these are opportunities to guide your children's growth, decision-making, and continued confidence in becoming adults. Keep in mind that when things go wrong, rather than saying, "I told you so," ask instead, "What did you learn from this experience, and how will it help your decision-making going forward?" Remember, there are no failures, just opportunities for children to learn from their mistakes. Start to embrace the multitude of "teachable moments" that you are given.

Help Your Child Have a Sense of Contribution

Let your children know what it means to you when they work with you on projects or household responsibilities. Sometimes we tend to dismiss the little things that we might say or do because they may feel too obvious or superfluous, but those words never are. Everyone benefits from sincere and genuine praise.

Help Your Child Make Real Choices and Decisions

You have reached that time when there will be some real choices and decisions to be made that can greatly affect your child's future. The more that you can allow teenagers to come to those choices and decisions on their own, the better. Your guidance and encouragement, advice, and support are an anchor, but if they are allowed to make the ultimate decisions, they will amass a tremendous sense of accomplishment that will position them to own their decisions and take responsibility for the outcomes.

Help Your Child Have a Sense of Self-discipline and Control

As teenagers mature and it is clearly appropriate to give them more independence, always remember to reinforce your expectations and guidelines clearly so teens continue to reflect, reason, problem solve, and consider the consequences of the actions they may choose in whatever scenario they face.

You may start the conversation with, "I am going to allow you to go to your friend's party. I expect that your friend's parents are home, and there will not be any drinking or drugs there. If anything should be different, I expect that you will leave or call me to come get you. I will not hold it against you if things do turn out differently than expected, as long as you make the choice to leave. I expect that you will never get into a car with a driver who has been drinking or is under the influence of any drugs. If I allow you to go to the party and find out afterward that things were different than you promised me, I will no longer have confidence that I can trust what you tell me, which will be a huge obstacle to your having more opportunities such as this one."

Help Your Child Have a Sense of Encouragement, Support, and Reward

Parenting can't always be about correcting or noticing what is wrong, even though there may be a lot that you could complain about through your child's adolescence. You may have asked your son a thousand times to clean his room and he never does it exactly as you would like. But when he picks up his socks and actually throws them in the hamper, say a word or two about how much you appreciate that. Say it often, say it clearly, and recognize those little things. Everyone responds better to positive reinforcement, so find those opportunities to build confidence and model appreciation.

Help Your Child Have a Sense of Family Belonging

Developing self-esteem begins within the family and is thus influenced greatly by the feelings and perceptions that family members have for each other. A sense of belonging is essential to self-esteem and can be nourished by consistent family mealtimes, encouraging each other's goals and activities, and caring for extended family members. Families gain confidence when the emphasis is on family strengths, avoiding excessive criticism, and sticking up for one another outside the family setting. Family and individual self-esteem are built when family members believe in and trust each other, respect each one's individual differences, and show affection for each other.

Instilling Healthy Attitudes

In 82% of US households, family members are sometimes or very often engaging in dieting activities. Family members are not immune to the effects of the media on self-image. Many teens do not believe that they are achieving or satisfying their own or their parents' expectations. One cause of this may be a result of their desire and need to constantly see how they measure up to friends and images that they see in the media. Images of famous celebrities, models, professional athletes, and others have no relevant comparison to the average person. To add insult to injury, these unrealistic media images are everywhere—on television, in movies and magazines, and on social media. We are exposed endlessly to people whose looks sometimes defy logic. Many images are in fact Photoshopped, but our kids don't realize or consider that. The blatant differences between these admired people and your child can trigger much distress and sometimes even lead to disordered eating behaviors and eating disorders. Build up your own self-esteem as a parent and help your teen to appreciate his or her individual strengths. Children's primary focus should be on who they are as a person and not on how they look. Parents are the models for their children in all things, so by practicing healthy self-care, you instill healthy attitudes in your child, which is a great gift to everyone.

American Culture and Its Influence on Adolescence

Understanding the relationship between perceived body image and self-esteem is important if we want to help adolescents. Americans have more issues with unhealthy weight than ever before, and yet the portrayal of the ideal body image for adults continues to be a body mass index (BMI) that is less than healthy. This fact plays a key role in the unhealthy self-image that many children have from a very young age.

Body Mass Index: What It Is

Body mass index, commonly referred to as BMI, is a calculation that pediatricians use to evaluate a child's weight status. To determine this number, they use the child's weight relative to height. Parents will find this useful when at the doctor's office with their child where a range will indicate whether their child is underweight, at a healthy weight, overweight, or has obesity.

The Barbie Doll, fashioned after a teenaged fashion model, made her debut in 1959 at the New York International Toy Fair. Barbie has become an icon of American culture, and it is doubtful that many American girls did not own at least one while growing up. Boys have had their hero, GI Joe, and subsequently other favorites like Batman and Superman. For both boys and girls, these beloved dolls have one important thing in common—their body type. Any child might be influenced to believe the dolls' body types are the ideal body type; however, the dolls' body types are absolutely nothing like those of the average American male or female teen!

When comparing Barbie and the average American woman, Barbie stands at an average height of 6 feet, weighing in at 101 pounds; her BMI is 13.74 (normal BMI is >18!). The average American woman is 5 feet 3.8 inches tall, 164.7 pounds, and has a BMI of 28.4 (which is in the overweight range). When we look at the dolls designed for men, we notice immediately that they have a muscular physique that is light-years from the average American male. As our developing boys and girls reach puberty, what do years of staring at, playing with, and idealizing the images of these figures do to their perception of self and what they feel they must attain to be beautiful?

The Centers for Disease Control and Prevention (CDC) National Health Statistics division compiled these and other data between 2003 and 2006. In 2008, the CDC launched its Body and Mind program activity, "If These Dolls Were Real People," which was used as a teaching tool for students to take measurements of popular dolls; those measurements were then projected to the actual size they would represent if the doll were a real person. The student could then appreciate the ridiculous differences between a real person's size and the size of the dolls that they grew up with.

Did you know that the average American woman is approximately 5'4" tall and weighs 165 pounds? This correlates with a BMI of 28.4. The average Miss America winner has a BMI of 16.9. The World Health Organization classifies a normal BMI as falling between 18.5 and 24.9. Talk to your child's pediatrician about what a realistic and healthy BMI looks like.

The Influence on Healthy Adolescent Development

The American Academy of Pediatrics estimates that kids see 40,000 television commercials each year, and they also are exposed to ads on the Internet, in magazines, on billboards, in newspapers, on the radio, and in other places. The effect of this on the developing brain and a child's self-image and how that shapes self-esteem is something parents and our adolescents must consider. We have a responsibility to take action and demand changes to the way in which our culture is shaped if we believe that aspects of that culture are unhealthy. Resources with information on fitness, nutrition, and positive body image are listed at the end of the chapter.

The CDC media literacy guide MediaSharps suggests that students and parents interested in learning about the effects of media on society should ask the following questions:

- Who is communicating and why?

- Who owns, profits from, and pays for media messages?

- How are media messages communicated?

- Who receives media messages, and what sense is made of them?

- What are the intended or underlying purposes, and whose point of view is behind the message?

- What is *not* being said and why?

- Is there consistency both within and across media?

Did you know that of the American elementary schoolgirls who read magazines, 69% say that the pictures influence their concept of the ideal body shape? Forty-seven percent say that the pictures make them want to lose weight. Parents can start conversations with their children on what they view as healthy and how they feel about images they see in the media. This can help a mom or dad see if their child's perception of healthy weight is skewed or not. These conversations can also be helpful with their pediatrician.

When an Unhealthy Body Image Leads to an Eating Disorder

Once robbed of a healthy self-image, harmful behaviors may develop in some vulnerable teens as they try to achieve their desired body image. An adolescent may have disordered eating, which is an unhealthy eating pattern such as skipping meals, restriction dieting, or compulsive eating, or he or she may have an eating disorder.

Eating disorders are complicated behavioral health problems that always require attention. The causes are varied, but a lack of self-esteem always plays a big role. Boys and girls both can be affected, although more girls than boys are usually diagnosed. Interestingly, eating disorders affect children of all weight categories. Parents should be concerned when any teen begins losing large amounts of weight rapidly, and this concern should be brought to the attention of the teen's pediatrician. When a child loses lots of weight rapidly, it can be a problem. What might appear to be a successful weight loss strategy on the surface might in fact represent an eating disorder. It is critical that weight loss be managed in a healthy way for children of all weight levels and at all ages, but this is especially true during puberty when rapid growth occurs.

Anorexia Nervosa

Anorexia nervosa affects between 0.5% and 1% of the women in the United States during their lifetime. About 15% of all cases of anorexia involve males. Some males are particularly uncomfortable with and ashamed about this diagnosis because they think that it is a female problem. Boys need to be reassured that there is absolutely no shame in struggling with an eating disorder of any type.

As an alternative to dieting, try looking online or in cookbooks for healthy meals that you can cook with your teen. Not only will you be spending quality time with one another, but you can decide together on what food to eat. Maybe there is something you both want to try. Are there vegetables you don't normally eat that could be incorporated into a meal where you would eat it? Make it fun!

Although more females than males are diagnosed with an eating disorder, an equal number of boys and girls exhibit disordered eating behaviors, which include binge eating, purging, laxative abuse, and fasting for weight loss. Many stereotypes about eating disorders exist, including the common belief that these disorders are a problem of wealthy, white adolescent females. The truth is that these disorders affect both genders and all ages, races, and socioeconomic classes. Any adolescent with rapid and/or excessive weight loss, vomiting or suspected vomiting, or possible depressive symptoms may have an eating disorder.

What Anorexia Looks Like

Teens with anorexia basically starve themselves. Their weight loss is never enough for them to feel satisfied with their body image, and they continue to restrict calories and often exercise to excess even when they are underweight. They have serious distortions of body image and will restrict calories even when their health is at risk. In an effort to accomplish their self-imposed weight management, children may commonly be deceitful to prove to those checking their weight that they are improving. Before being weighed, they might drink water in huge amounts or try to hide a heavy object on their persons to fake weight gain or hide further weight loss. Affected teens are completely consumed with accomplishing more and more weight loss. This often leads to nutritional deficiencies, sleep problems, constipation, and the inability to think rationally about their own well-being.

Anorexia is a life-threatening problem that requires early recognition and immediate intervention. One of the most notable signs of anorexia is the child's lack of concern and disregard for the gravity of the problem. Preoccupation with food is intense and severe. Parents often will remark about the way in which their child "plays" with food, often pushing it around the plate incessantly and taking an inordinate amount of time to eat the tiniest amount. Parents also may notice that their teen is depressed.

The following are the hallmarks of anorexia:

- Intense preoccupation with food

- Severe weight loss

- A family history of eating disorders

- Severe food restrictive behaviors, vomiting, and excessive exercise

- Complete denial about the problem

- Behaving in a withdrawn and asexual manner (no affinity for sexuality)

- Two common periods of onset—ages 13 to 14 years and 17 to 18 years

- A very slow heart rate, low blood pressure, and heart arrhythmias

- Depressed, sometimes suicidal, mood; possible obsessional fears

- In girls, delayed menstruation or stopping menstruation once begun

- Lower than normal body temperature

- Possible hypercarotenemia (a yellow-orange complexion)

- Hair loss

- Lanugo (the development of very fine body hair, predominantly on the back)

Denial About Anorexia

Teens, and sometimes parents, tend to dismiss the seriousness of a teen's weight loss and preoccupation with food. Often, the teen will refuse to discuss the situation and the possibility of treatment. Teens with anorexia may implore you not to enter them into treatment, but instead let them work on their weight management alone. They may insist that things may have gotten a bit out of control, but they have a handle on their weight loss and eating and will be able to turn things around if you let them. This rational discussion may lull you into thinking that your teen's problem is not as serious as it is. However, the likelihood that a teen with anorexia will get better without special treatment is practically nonexistent. If there is a possibility that your child has an eating problem, discussing this with your child's pediatrician is absolutely critical. Anorexia is a dangerous condition that can cause lifelong health repercussions and even death.

Talking With Your Teen About Anorexia

You may believe that you can supervise your teen's eating behaviors and move your teen back to regular eating habits and patterns. But most of the time that is not feasible. Demonstrating confidence in a teen with anorexia seems positive because it allows the teen to have the responsibility of working out his or her problems independently. But delaying treatment can have serious consequences. The bottom line is that what may appear to be a manageable circumstance to you and your teen is hardly that. This is a disease that, if left untreated, carries a very real risk of death. When death occurs, it is usually because of heart rhythm problems or severe complications of electrolyte imbalances.

If you believe that there is a chance that your son or daughter might have an eating disorder, you must bring it up with your teen's pediatrician. It is not uncommon for parents whose children are diagnosed as having anorexia will remark later that they had had suspicions but didn't want to jump to conclusions. Be brave and speak up! If you are wrong, that is OK. But if your suspicions are correct, you may save your child's life.

Early, appropriate treatment is imperative. Anorexia nervosa has the highest mortality rate of any psychiatric illness. And for girls between ages 15 and 24 years, the mortality rate is 12 times higher than the death rate of all other causes of death. I recommend you begin your conversation with statements rather than questions because teens with anorexia are generally not forthcoming. More often they are deceitful about their actions, either due to embarrassment or concern over admitting they have a problem. Asking a question may not yield the truth, so state the facts. Inform your teen of the behaviors that you notice, such as losing unhealthy amounts of weight, eating minimally or avoiding meals altogether, or loss of interest in family and friends. Next, reassure your teen that you are going to help. Many teens who have anorexia want to be helped but fear they cannot be helped. This disorder is best managed by a team approach with skilled professionals. Assure your teen that he or she will be OK, and you will get through this together as a family. Your teen may be relieved or become very argumentative. He or she may tell you that you do not know what you are talking about. Stay calm, stand your ground, and do not get into an argument, no matter how mad your teen may seem. Let your teen know that as the parent, your priority is to look out for his or her health and well-being.

Bulimia

Bulimia is eating an amount of food that is definitely larger than most would eat, within a relatively short period, usually within 2 hours or less, and then inducing vomiting. One in 5 ninth graders and 2 in 5 high school seniors admit to at least once stuffing themselves with food and then forcing themselves to vomit. Up to 1 in 4 US teenagers binge and purge regularly. If this continues for 3 months, the young person is said to be bulimic.

What Bulimia Looks Like

Many children with anorexia have episodes of bulimia at one time or another. Bulimia is also a disorder of distorted body image with an obsession to slim down. Different things trigger bingeing behavior. Adolescents with this disorder will eat until they cannot eat anymore, then experience feelings of overwhelming guilt and shame, often resulting in purging behaviors to rid themselves of the calories. This might be done by self-induced vomiting, usually by sticking their fingers down their throat, or the misuse of laxatives, diuretics, or other products. Contrary to what the child with bulimia believes, this behavior does not aid in weight control or weight loss. Most children with bulimia gain weight over time.

> Did you know that girls who diet frequently are 12 times more likely to binge as girls who don't diet? Dieting is not always the healthiest way to manage weight and may not be recommended. Talk with your teen's pediatrician about various ways for your child to eat healthy and ways to incorporate physical activity into his or her daily routine. Make sure to include your teen in this conversation!

Some kids may have other means of elimination, such as taking large amounts of laxatives to increase and speed up the amount of stool produced, diuretics to increase urine production, or emetics to force vomiting. Children with bulimia will plan carefully for this behavior and do it all secretly. This can take a very negative toll on their health, severely affecting the kidneys, liver, intestines, and heart. Electrolyte abnormalities, especially with potassium, can result in death, just as for teens with anorexia.

Eating Behavior Warning Signs

The following are some warnings that you can look out for:

- Preoccupation with food

- A distorted body image, often accompanied by frequent checking of oneself in the mirror for perceived flaws

- Spending long periods in the bathroom, especially after eating— sometimes running the water to drown out the sound of vomiting

- Depression, irritability, or intense mood swings

- Anxiety about eating and unhealthy dieting habits, often described as *clean eating,* with elimination of total food groups such as dairy, carbs, sugar, and fat or meat without paying close attention to satisfying nutritional requirements

- Food rituals, such as cutting food into tiny pieces, chewing an inordinate amount of times, or eating unusually slowly

- Using laxatives, enemas, diuretics, or emetics

- Spending less time with family and friends; becoming more isolated, secretive (eating secretly), and acting withdrawn

- Stealing food and hoarding it in unusual places, such as in a closet or under the bed

- Excitability; has difficultly sitting still, is easily distracted, exercises excessively even when ill

Some of the physical changes that can occur include

- Dramatic weight fluctuations that come from alternately dieting and bingeing

- Major changes in attitude and behavior about food, size, weight, and basic self-image
- Puffy face and throat from swollen salivary glands
- Burst blood vessels in the face
- Bags under the eyes
- Indigestion, bloating, constipation, gas pains, abdominal cramps
- Dehydration
- Eroded tooth enamel from the gastric acid in vomit; discolored teeth
- Cavities
- Inflamed, bleeding gums (gingivitis)
- Calluses on fingers and knuckles from self-induced vomiting
- Swelling (edema) of the feet or hands
- Sore throat
- Tremors
- Dizziness, light-headedness, or fainting spells
- Stiff, achy muscles
- Muscle weakness
- Muscle cramps
- Irregular menstruation
- Extreme thirst and frequent urination
- A constant sensation of feeling cold, especially in the hands and feet, because the body has lost its "overcoat" of fat and muscle (if the teen is underweight)
- Hair loss
- Blurred vision

Teens with bulimia are generally at average or above-average weight and, as a result, are often able to hide their condition for years. As with anorexia, making the diagnosis and getting the person into treatment is critical and can be lifesaving.

One resource for help is the National Eating Disorder Association. Its hotline number is 800/931-2237. If you would prefer instant messaging instead of calling the hotline, there is a click-to-chat option to connect with a trained helpline volunteer on its Web site (**https://www. nationaleatingdisorders.org**).

Talking With Your Teen About Bulimia

Parents who fear their teen has bulimia must address this head on. It is unlikely that their child will admit to any of the dysfunctional eating or purging behaviors, unless discovered by their parents. And if so, their child may stress that it was a one-time thing and won't happen again. On the other hand, your teen may argue and insist that the problem isn't that serious, that you don't understand, and that he or she only wants to be left alone. Don't engage in an argument or allow yourself to get rattled. Stay calm and in control and do your best to not take your teen's emotions or words personally.

The extreme weight loss in teens who have anorexia is a major indicator of their disorder; however, those with bulimia can have a healthy-looking weight or little to no obvious weight loss, which may hide the fact that a problem is present. If you are convinced that there is a health concern, trust your gut. Parents always know best! No one knows your child better than you. The biggest mistake that a parent can make is to allow the teen to have space. He or she may make threats, so be ready to sit down with your teen and tell him or her that you are going to get the help that is needed. Explicitly explain to your teen that you know something is very wrong, but you love him or her and will find the proper help. The only thing that you must do is follow through and get him or her to the immediate care that he or she needs.

A Time of Rapid Change

Parenting through puberty is demanding, and it is never more demanding and difficult than when trying to encourage your teen to feel good about him- or herself. Puberty by definition is a time of rapid changes regarding the body, mind, and emotions. Without the turmoil of puberty, the average person, or even child for that matter, often battles with feelings of insecurities about body image. What happens when your body starts to change, the brain begins to work differently, and your emotions are affected by an influx of new hormones? It doesn't seem surprising that while going through puberty, one's concept of body image is put to the test. The big question is what do we as parents do to support the health and well-being of our teens as they travel through puberty?

Never take for granted how much your love and support mean to your adolescent. While growth is moving at this rapid pace and your teen's temperament may now resemble a roller-coaster ride, remember that your teen needs and loves you, even in the moments that he or she appears to have forgotten this fact! You need to rise above the obnoxious moments and see the big picture: your child is becoming an adult.

The road to adulthood is paved with uneven breasts, pubic hair, pimples, extra fat cells, and raging hormones. It's not always pretty, figuratively and literally! So, remind your children that they are beautiful. They are on a new adventure, and time will heal some of the insecurities of the moment. Everyone who has ever been through puberty can relate. Keep your children grounded and focused on the person inside and the great changes still to come.

Resources

American Academy of Pediatrics. Eating disorders: bulimia.
HealthyChildren.org Web site. **https://www.healthychildren.org/
English/health-issues/conditions/emotional-problems/Pages/Eating-
Disorders-Bulimia.aspx**. Updated November 21, 2015.
Accessed May 8, 2018

Body Positive. Boosting body image at any weight.
http://www.bodypositive.com. Accessed May 8, 2018
This Web site seeks to boost well-being, self-esteem, and positive body image
at any healthy weight. The site offers resources, activism issues, forums, and
strategies to help people find acceptance for their body weight concerns.

CANFIT. Communities, adolescents, nutrition, fitness.
http://www.canfit.org. Accessed May 8, 2018
The California Adolescent Nutrition and Fitness Program provides
resources on adolescent nutrition and body image, fitness, and more.
It is oriented toward adolescents in low-income communities and
communities of color.

The Center for Eating Disorders at Sheppard Pratt. Bulimia nervosa.
https://eatingdisorder.org/eating-disorder-information/bulimia-nervosa.
Accessed May 8, 2018

Centers for Disease Control and Prevention. If those dolls were real people.
https://www.cdc.gov/bam/teachers/documents/body_image_dolls.pdf.
Accessed May 8, 2018

Hispanic Access Foundation. Powerful Bones. Powerful Girls. The National
Bone Health Campaign.
**https://www.hispanicaccess.org/service-provider-directory/powerful-
bones-powerful-girls-national-bone-health-campaign**. Accessed
May 8, 2018
The CDC Powerful Bones, Powerful Girls is a national health campaign
sponsored by the Office of Women's Health that provides tips on healthy
eating and physical activity.

National Eating Disorders Association. What are eating disorders? **https://www.nationaleatingdisorders.org/sites/default/files/ ResourceHandouts/GeneralStatistics.pdf**. Accessed May 8, 2018

National Institute of Diabetes and Digestive and Kidney Diseases, National Institutes of Health. Sisters together. **https://www.niddk.nih.gov/health-information/professionals/ materials/sisters-together**. Accessed May 8, 2018
Sisters Together Program Guide: Move More, Eat Better is a national initiative to encourage African American women to maintain a healthy weight by becoming more physically active and eating healthier foods.

National Institute of Diabetes and Digestive and Kidney Diseases, National Institutes of Health. Take charge of your health: a guide for teenagers. **https://www.niddk.nih.gov/health-information/ weight-management/take-charge-health-guide-teenagers**. Published December 2016. Accessed May 8, 2018
The Weight-control Information Network, an information service of the National Institute of Diabetes and Digestive and Kidney Diseases, National Institutes of Health, was established in 1994 to provide the general public, health professionals, the media, and Congress with up-to-date, science-based information on obesity, weight control, physical activity, positive body image, and related nutritional issues. "Take Charge of Your Health: A Guide for Teenagers" focuses on healthy eating, physical activity, and how to make successful changes in a teen's daily life.

Neumark-Sztainer D. *I'm, Like, SO Fat! Helping Your Teen Make Healthy Choices about Eating and Exercise in a Weight-Obsessed World*. New York, NY: Guilford Press; 2005

Office on Women's Health. girlshealth.gov. **https://www.girlshealth.gov**. Accessed May 8, 2018
The Office on Women's Health provides girls with reliable health information on physical activity, nutrition, and stress reduction.

President's Council on Sports, Fitness, and Nutrition.
https://www.hhs.gov/fitness/index.html. Accessed May 8, 2018
The President's Council on Sports, Fitness, and Nutrition provides
regular updates on the council's activities as well as resources on
how to get involved in its programs.

TeensHealth from Nemours. Body image and self-esteem.
http://kidshealth.org/en/teens/body-image.html. Reviewed July 2015.
Accessed May 8, 2018
The Nemours Foundation is an information resource for teens focused
on the development of positive body image and self-esteem.

US Department of Agriculture. ChooseMyPlate.gov.
https://www.choosemyplate.gov. Accessed May 8, 2018
US Department of Agriculture food guidance system that contains
general recommendations including food checklists, information on
a healthy eating style, physical activity, online tools, and other topics.

US Department of Agriculture Food and Nutrition Service.
Team Nutrition. **https://www.fns.usda.gov/tn/team-nutrition**.
Published April 20, 2018. Accessed May 8, 2018
The US Department of Agriculture Team Nutrition Web site focuses
on the role nutritious school meals, nutrition education, and a health-
promoting school environment play in helping students learn to enjoy
healthy eating and physical activity.

Wertheim E, Paxton S, Blaney S. Body image in girls. In: Smolak L,
Thompson JK, eds. *Body Image, Eating Disorders, and Obesity in Youth:
Assessment, Prevention, and Treatment.* 2nd ed. Washington, DC:
American Psychological Association; 2009:47–76

Zernike K. Sizing up America: signs of expansion from head to toe.
The New York Times. **http://www.nytimes.com/2004/03/01/us/
sizing-up-america-signs-of-expansion-from-head-to-toe.html**.
Published March 1, 2004. Accessed May 8, 2018

CHAPTER 3

Variations of Puberty Growth and Growing Pains

When you became a parent, you probably thought, secretly, that your baby was the cutest baby that had ever been born. As parents we know we are not supposed to compare, but it is hard not to! We are so in love with these little miracles, we can't help thinking our little one is the most miraculous.

As your child grows, you may notice, however, that he or she is not the first one to talk or the first one to walk or ride a bike compared with the other kids at child care. Every child is unique and you find that the moments to celebrate are often not the ones in which your child is first, but moments in which he or she achieved a personal victory.

Even though the stages of puberty are quite similar, it is best not to compare when children begin puberty because it is so different for all children. The age at which your child will begin puberty depends on many factors, including genetics. Understanding that your child's maturation can vary from other children's without being concerned is important.

Some situations, however, can be considered unusual and require a trip to the pediatrician. A doctor should see your child if the first signs of puberty are apparent before age 8 years in girls and age 9 years in boys. Also, if girls have no signs of breast development by age 13 years or no periods by 15 years, they should be seen by a doctor. Similarly, if a boy shows no signs of puberty by age 14 years, he should be seen by a doctor.

Early Puberty

When children are young, they look in awe at older kids and young adults, and they often fantasize about how wonderful it would be to have a mature body and mind, as well as all the imagined privileges of those years. However, when maturation actually begins, it is not always celebrated as the wonderful gateway to adulthood that we appreciate in hindsight. In fact, most children feel quite awkward and uncomfortable as they pass through the stages of puberty.

Awkward as it is for tweens to begin puberty, it can feel worse if they are changing earlier than most of their peers. You may have heard this referred to as being an early bloomer. Tweens and adolescents find solace in their sameness, and, ironically, your child might claim to be an independent doer and thinker, but might still look uncannily like his or her peers. At this age, boldly differentiating oneself might be like having a different color of the same pair of jeans worn by nearly every child in school!

The awkwardness, clumsiness, and weight gain that signal the beginning of puberty are changes that are entirely expected. Even though your tween may not necessarily want to discuss puberty with peers, he or she can at least see that others are going through quite similar physical changes. If it appears that your child is changing all alone, he or she can be feeling lonely, scared, out of place, and miserable. It is important that your child talks to someone who can help him or her understand these feelings and not feel alone. Your child's pediatrician can also help answer any questions you or your child may have.

Talking About Body Changes

Parents should be sensitive to the fact that many children will not independently talk about the changes that they are going through and the way it is affecting them. Children benefit from discussing their feelings about these changes; an opportunity for discussion allows them to ask questions that they may be too unsure to otherwise ask.

The kinds of questions that girls who go through puberty before other girls might ask include

- Why does it hurt when I bump into things?
- Will the pain ever stop?
- Why is this happening to me?
- Is this cancer? (referring to breast bud)
- Why am I different from my friends?
- Am I OK?
- Will this happen to my friends?

Usually, girls are the ones most disturbed by developing early because boys are often excited about the changes that puberty brings. But what happens usually is not what happens always, so parents of both boys and girls who are developing early might begin a conversation about puberty changes by saying "Do you know what puberty means? Have you heard of puberty? Puberty is the word that we use to describe how our bodies change from a child to an adult. Have you ever wondered how that happens?" Allow your child to ask questions; usually, they don't have many if they are quite young when puberty begins.

You may also consider discussing how different your daughter might feel from those who have not yet started developing. "You know, I see that you are starting to develop. Most girls your age who start to develop a little early have some worries about this. Do you have any worries?" Keep the channels of communication open and express a willingness to discuss all the emotions that your daughter might be experiencing. Don't be afraid to come out and say, "I'm so glad that we got to speak with the doctor about how your body is starting to go through some changes. How are you feeling about that?" You can mention that you know she is developing a bit earlier than many of her friends and understand that it may make her feel uncomfortable, but there certainly isn't anything wrong with being an early bloomer and she can feel comfortable talking with you if she needs to. Girls often develop in a similar fashion as their mothers, which gives their mothers an opportunity to mention things from that standpoint: "When I was about your age, I started to go through changes that I wasn't sure that I understood. How can I help you to better understand what is happening?"

Even though a mom might have an easier time discussing this with her daughter because she can relate to the body changes, a dad can and should feel confident addressing these topics with his daughter as well. Fathers should let their daughters know in the same way that moms can with their sons that while they cannot relate exactly to the changes, they are here to listen and help as needed. Offering books on puberty and body changes and discussing what they read can be helpful for both parents and their child. Including another family member of the same gender as your child in these conversations can also help everyone understand the changes happening and offer any guidance or help that your child might need. Reassurance is just as comforting from your same sex parent as from the opposite sex parent. Be understanding, be kind, be patient.

Growing Pains

Many parents ask, "Are growing pains a real thing?" Yes, there really is something called growing pains. These often begin in both boys and girls between ages 3 and 5 years and may return between ages 8 and 11 years. Occasionally, growing pains continue into puberty.

Children will often complain of pain in their shins, their calves, the front part of their thighs, or behind their knees; very rarely, their arms may be affected. These pains tend to be worse in the early evening, but occasionally a child will awaken and complain of it. Once the pain has begun, it may return over the next several days and then stop abruptly. Massaging the area can often ease the soreness.

Parents may be nervous if their child experiences this pain, but there is no reason to be. The pain should never cause your child to limp. Your child's muscles, bones, nerves, or joints should not be affected. If your tween or teen is suffering and you have concerns, always check with your pediatrician.

Staying Vigilant

Some children may feel ashamed or embarrassed about their body changes and now refuse to be engaged in activities that they previously enjoyed. They may feel embarrassed that their peers are not transitioning through puberty and may be very aware of the differences in their bodies. They might feel they are being placed in compromising situations, such as needing to change in public locker rooms alongside their peers. Asking the right questions in a compassionate, nonjudgmental, and nonthreatening manner is important. Either parent can begin with conversation starters such as, "I've noticed each week there is a different reason you need to miss swim practice, and I can't help but think that something is bothering you. Is there a reason you don't want to go anymore?" If you get a shrug, try being a little more direct. "I know that you have started to have some grown-up changes in your body and I know that can be a reason to not want to be around other kids in the locker room. Do you think that might be what is bothering you?"

Keep vigilant for signs of difficulties in your child's emotional development and exercise a great deal of sensitivity in asking and answering questions. "I've noticed that you seem to be very sensitive these days about things, and I want you to know that I am concerned about how you are feeling. If it has something to do with the changes that are going on with your body, I would love to listen to you. I will do my best to help and we can work together on whatever is troubling you."

Is It Really Puberty?

Sometimes when a girl carries extra weight, she can appear to have full breasts even though she has not yet entered puberty. Fat is different than breast tissue. The breast contour will likely look different with fat than with actual breast tissue. To determine whether puberty has begun in a young girl, it may be necessary for the doctor to look for other signs of puberty, such as the presence of pubic hair.

However, this does not always answer the question of whether puberty has begun because it is possible that the child does have *thelarche,* a condition in which breasts develop even though puberty is not occurring. Noticing your daughter's shoe size may help you determine whether puberty has begun. If it has recently changed greatly, the growth spurt is beginning and likely means that puberty is underway.

In a girl younger than 8 years, puberty is not typical, and a doctor needs to examine her to see if there is anything that needs to be addressed.

Delayed Puberty

When a child begins puberty late, parents should take note. It is painful to look no older than age 9 years when you are 13! (See Figure 3-1.) Some parents are alarmed by the fact that their tween's development is delayed compared with peers, and some parents seem oblivious. Often, the oblivious parent is one who developed with a similar pattern. It is important to recognize that a child developing late probably has some concerns even if he or she is not voicing them. Kids often worry in silence. They are often very relieved to find out that the delay in their maturation has no medical implications and that they will catch up. School physicals sometimes offer an opportunity for your teen to talk about concerns independently with the pediatrician or staff. A talk with the pediatrician may help the teenager and parents better understand what is happening.

Talking With Your Teen About Delayed Puberty

Parents often shy away from certain topics because they aren't sure of what to say and sometimes believe they will call attention to something that may only worsen the situation. Often, it is the unknown, the fear of what might be wrong, that is the greatest source of worry for parents, children, and teens.

Children who are experiencing delayed pubertal development need to have their fears handled. Discussing these fears with them will not make the situation worse but, rather, will allow them to better accept what is happening and understand that eventually they will experience the changes that come with puberty.

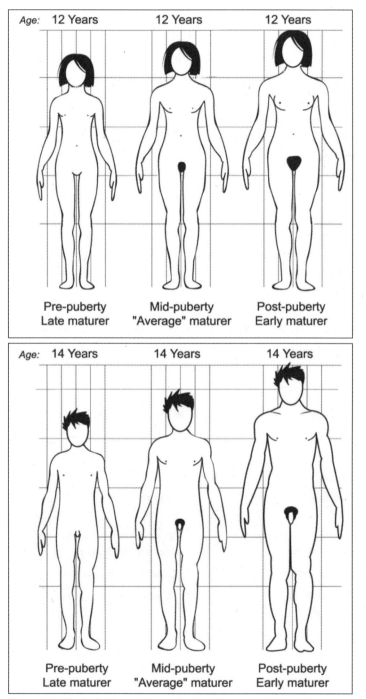

Figure 3-1. The Early Bloomer Versus the Late Bloomer in Girls and Boys
Adapted with permission. Copyright © (1973) Scientific American, a division of Nature America, Inc. All rights reserved.

Mention to your teen that you are aware that his or her growth is slower than his or her friends and ask if this is a comfortable conversation to have with you. Tell your teen that you understand and appreciate that growing differently is a very difficult stage to go through. Share some of your own experiences with your teen. Teens often feel that they are alone with this problem, and your teen may be surprised to learn that you went through this too. Keep in mind that although your experiences may help your teen to some extent, his or her reality may be quite different than yours. Stay empathetic, patient, and kind. Ask about your teen's concerns and try to address them. If you are unable to address them, offer to bring those concerns to your teen's doctor to discuss in greater detail. If your teen chooses not to talk about these concerns, try bringing up the topic again in a few weeks. Once you have emphasized that you are available to help, your teen may feel more comfortable opening up at a later time.

You should speak with the doctor if your son is 14 and shows no signs of puberty, if your daughter is 13 and shows no signs of breast development, or if your daughter is 15 and has not begun to menstruate.

Signs of Delayed Puberty in Boys

- Physically smaller than other children his age.
- Facial features are still delicate looking.
- Body type is childlike, lacking any "filled-out" features.
- Hands and feet are small.
- Voice is without maturation.
- No new hair growth anywhere.
- Many interests remain childlike.

Signs of Delayed Puberty in Girls

- Physically smaller than other children her age.
- Facial features are still delicate looking.
- Body type is childlike and lacks "bumps and curves."
- Hands and feet are small.
- Interests remain childlike.

Low Body Fat

Girls and boys alike can have what is called *constitutional growth delay,* which simply means puberty has been delayed for unknown reasons. However, they can also have delayed puberty because of very low body fat. Girls, particularly, who are highly athletic in sports such as gymnastics, competitive swimming, and ballet are commonly affected. It is not uncommon that the beginning of menstruation is delayed when body fat is very low. Also, when girls have eating disorders such as anorexia nervosa, extreme dieting, or bingeing and purging, puberty is often affected (see Chapter 2).

Delayed Puberty Tips

Plan a trip to the mall to buy your daughter a training bra. Spend some time getting a manicure and pedicure, grabbing lunch, chatting, and sharing this time together. Growing up slowly means you have more time to get ready, which can be lots of fun! Include grandmothers, aunts, sisters, or any other friends or family members that would enjoy this outing and help make your child feel more comfortable with where she is in the growing process.

Encourage physical activities for your son that are not dependent on a muscular frame, such as swimming or running, and in which he can excel now. Emphasize that he can train and polish his skills and technique now for participation in sports later on. It will help him tremendously when he finally gets his growth spurt. Consider letting him style his hair in an appropriate yet contemporary fashion or allow him to purchase his own style of clothes when out shopping so he can feel more comfortable with his appearance.

Chronic Illnesses and Conditions

Some chronic illnesses and conditions can be the cause of delayed puberty. These could include recurrent infections, immune system deficiencies, gastrointestinal (GI) illnesses, kidney problems, respiratory illnesses, anemia, endocrine disorders, or eating disorders. Sometimes the problem might worsen if it is poorly managed. If this is suspected, your child's pediatrician will choose the appropriate tests to determine the cause.

Performance-enhancing Substances

In some cases, teens who are concerned about their delay in puberty will consider trying unhealthy products such as performance-enhancing substances (PES) in the hope of promoting and enhancing their development. Adolescents may use dietary supplements and steroids to improve their appearance. Most adolescents are more interested in using these products to enhance their appearance than to affect athletic performance. Late bloomers are especially at risk because they often believe that using PES can influence their pubertal development. Many PES are sold over the counter as dietary supplements. As supplements, they do not require US Food and Drug Administration approval. Many parents and the athletes who choose to use these compounds are unaware of this lack of oversight. These products can possibly be contaminated with prohibited substances or can sometimes be missing active ingredients. Several studies that tested protein supplements revealed that 8% to 20% of these products were contaminated with significant amounts of heavy metals. These products are best to be avoided, plain and simple.

Many studies have shown that although overall use of many substances by adolescents has decreased, use of PES remains common in children and adolescents. Throughout adolescence, the use of all PES tends to go up with age and becomes greater in athletes than nonathletes.

Research has shown a correlation between use of PES and the use of alcohol and drugs, as well as other risk-taking behaviors. For most young athletes, using such substances does not create any more gains in strength and performance than what would occur during the onset of puberty with proper nutrition and appropriate athletic training.

What Adolescents Are Using

The most common PES used by adolescents are protein supplements, creatine, and caffeine.

Protein Supplements

The following are the groups of preteens and teens that predominantly consume protein supplements and the amounts they consume:

- Middle school girls: 25%

- Middle school boys: 30%

- High school girls: 18%

- High school boys: 39%

The products are consumed in a variety of powders, bars, and shakes. They are used mostly because kids believe that these supplements will provide building blocks for muscle and lean tissue growth to be replenished and supported. However, there is no performance benefit from these supplements if diet provides adequate protein. Eating adequate protein from natural food sources is preferred by the medical community, and, as stated earlier, there is a risk of contamination with these products.

Creatine

Creatine is a compound that occurs naturally in the body. Creatine is also sold as an over-the-counter supplement used to improve performance during high-intensity bursts of activity, as well as to increase muscle mass and strength. However, no benefits have generally been shown in aerobic activities or with on-field athletic performance. Short-term use at suggested doses appears to be safe in normal adults; however, the safety of supplemental creatine has not been evaluated specifically in adolescents. Creatine may have a negative effect on the kidneys, and it should not be used at all in any adolescent who may be at risk for kidney problems. In addition, when creatine is used for endurance activities rather than short-term activity, the kidneys do not work as well.

Caffeine

Caffeine is the active ingredient in coffee, but it can be found in many other products, such as sodas, energy drinks, and other dietary supplements. The US Food and Drug Administration regulates the amount of caffeine in soft drinks, allowing a maximum of 71 mg per 12 oz, but that is not the case with energy drinks or supplements. The harmful effects of consuming caffeine include cardiac arrhythmias (abnormal contractions of the heart), an increase in blood pressure, headaches, irritability, sleep disruption, tremor, gastric irritation, and increased core temperature when exercising. Serious toxic overload occurs when anyone consumes multiple energy drinks, and this practice led to almost 1,500 emergency department visits in the United States in 2011 in the 12- to 17-year age group. In their clinical report, "Sports Drinks and Energy Drinks for Children and Adolescents: Are They Appropriate?" the Committee on Nutrition and the Council on Sports Medicine and Fitness of the American Academy of Pediatrics (AAP) specifically state that energy drinks containing stimulants should never be consumed by children and adolescents.

What Adolescents Don't Know

Adolescents are unaware that when the effects of the hormones that are produced during puberty are paired with proper athletic training, the results will yield great athletic and muscular improvements. This is even more pronounced as the growth spurt reaches its peak. While using PES, most adolescents will not appreciate the same improvements that they will get by paying attention to a nutritious diet and training with proper fundamentals during puberty. Products containing PES are not a "shortcut" to enhanced athletic performance. As stated earlier, there is a risk of using contaminated products and having a lack of the desired active ingredient in PES.

What Might Contribute to Teen Use of Performance-enhancing Substances

- Dissatisfaction with the body
- Having a higher body mass index
- Training in a commercial gym
- Exposure to appearance-oriented fitness media
- Alcohol or drug use
- Engaging in other risk-taking behaviors

Talking to Your Teen About PES

Begin by asking permission to discuss the important topic of PES. This may be difficult to do, but it is worth it. Your teen may try to avoid the conversation completely or try to stress to you that it is not a big deal; however, you need to emphasize that you feel strongly about talking about it. Once you have the green light, let your teen know that the purpose of this talk has nothing to do with your attitude toward PES, but everything to do with his or her health and well-being. Explain that false information is easily spread, and you want your teen to know the truth about what these substances are and how they could affect his or her body. Educate yourself about the specific PES in question so you can relay this information and the reasons you are worried about your teen using them. If you find that this is too difficult to express without your teen becoming defensive, consider approaching this topic at another time or suggesting that this be a conversation to have with another family member, a counselor, or your teen's pediatrician.

Bullying

Children who are different from, smaller, or weaker than their peers often are targets of bullying. Targets could be children who develop early or children who are late to develop. Children who are developing late may lag a bit in emotional, as well as physical, development. We know that bullies look for children who exhibit signs of weakness.

The following are several forms that bullying can take:

- Physical abuse—hitting, kicking, pushing, punching

- Verbal—threatening, taunting, teasing, hate speech

- Cyberbullying—online targeting, sometimes anonymously and other times via public humiliation (eg, a video of the target posted on the Internet without consent)

- Social—excluding targets from activities or starting rumors about them

- Cyber harassment—online bullying of a child by an adult

If your child is the target of bullying, take it seriously. Children who are bullied are at greater risk for low self-esteem, depression, and suicide. Specific steps that you as a parent can take to help and protect your child include

- Talk with your child about bullying. Even an older child may know very little about what drives bullying behavior. Ask specifically about whether your child has been the recipient of bullying.

- Help your child learn effective ways to respond and cope.

  - Ignore the bully as much as possible.

  - Don't let the bully see that you are upset.

  - Respond firmly and definitively, "Leave me alone."

  - Encourage your child to speak up when help is needed.

  - Keep existing friends close and keep those bonds strong.

  - Alert school officials if bullying behavior is present.

Often, older children believe that somehow the bullying is their fault, or they feel ashamed that they have been targeted and find it difficult to bring up and discuss. If your child stops wanting to go to school, starts having new and regular aches and pains, or has grades that are starting to slip, consider the possibility of bullying. This can happen with any teen, but children with growth variation are more vulnerable simply because of the different, obvious way in which they grow.

For more information on bullying, see Chapter 5 and the Resources section at the end of this chapter.

Appreciating the Differences

Parenting your child through puberty can be challenging. Although typical, growing at different times and rates than other children and adolescents can create a problem. Maturing early is one obstacle and maturing later is another. Perceptive and understanding parents can anticipate some of the insecurities that often accompany growth concerns, no matter what the timing. This is especially important in regard to the use of many PES. Although their general use may have appeared to have declined over the past 15 years, multiple studies have now prompted concern that adolescent use of these substances is on the increase. Parents and pediatricians can help adolescents be secure in their own pattern of growth and help them navigate puberty contentedly, confidently, and safely without these products.

Resources

American Academy of Pediatrics. A Minute for Kids: quitting a sports program. HealthyChildren.org Web site. **http://www.healthychildren.org/ English/healthy-living/sports/Pages/Quitting-a-Sports-Program.aspx**. Published January 16, 2016. Accessed May 8, 2018

American Academy of Pediatrics. Bullying: it's not OK. HealthyChildren.org Web site. **https://www.healthychildren.org/ English/safety-prevention/at-play/Pages/Bullying-Its-Not-Ok.aspx**. Updated November 21, 2015. Accessed May 8, 2018

American Academy of Pediatrics. How you can help your child avoid & address bullying. HealthyChildren.org Web site. **https://www. healthychildren.org/ English/safety-prevention/at-play/Pages/Avoiding-Bullying.aspx**. Updated November 21, 2015. Accessed May 8, 2018

Korioth T. Signs of bullying: important questions for parents to ask. American Academy of Pediatrics HealthyChildren.org Web site. **https://www.healthychildren.org/English/safety-prevention/at-play/ Pages/Bullies-Beat-Down-Self-Esteem.aspx**. Published January 22, 2016. Accessed May 8, 2018

Kowal-Connelly S. When the early & late bloomer meet up in sports: tips for parents & coaches. American Academy of Pediatrics HealthyChildren. org Web site. **http://www.healthychildren.org/English/ages-stages/ teen/fitness/Pages/Sports-Goals-and-Applications-Teens.aspx**. Published July 29, 2016. Accessed May 8, 2018

Mayo Clinic. Healthy lifestyle: tween and teen health. Performance-enhancing drugs and teen athletes. **https://www.mayoclinic.org/ healthy-lifestyle/tween-and-teen-health/in-depth/performance-enhancing-drugs/art-20046620**. Published March 22, 2018. Accessed May 8, 2018

Moreno M. Cyberbullying. American Academy of Pediatrics HealthyChildren.org Web site. **https://www.healthychildren.org/ English/family-life/Media/Pages/Cyberbullying.aspx**. Updated January 27, 2018. Accessed May 8, 2018

PART

The Emotional Changes

CHAPTER 4

Understanding the Emotional and Intellectual Stages of Puberty

As your teen makes his or her way through the emotional stages of puberty, you may find yourself questioning many aspects of parenthood. Typical questions include

- Should I be concerned about the changes in my child?

- Does everyone go through this trouble with their child?

- Does my child hate me?

- Did I do something wrong to cause this turmoil?

- Will I always feel sad about missing the way my child was before puberty?

- Will I ever have a close and meaningful relationship with my child again?

Parents may have just as much trouble navigating this period as their child does, and maybe even more. One day you wake up and your angelic child has been replaced by a venom-lipped intruder. In fairness, puberty presents countless challenges for teens as well as their parents. It is helpful to understand these behaviors as inevitable occurrences directly related to stages of human development. It's the natural progression of life, and everyone experiences these developmental traumas. Most importantly, these are necessary changes that help shape your teen into the independent adult that he or she will ultimately become.

Understanding and anticipating the emotional growth associated with puberty can reduce a parent's anxiety; the teenager/parent conflict is universal. If your misery wants company, you have it.

Regardless of who you are or where you come from, adolescent development and adolescent/parental conflicts occur predictably and consistently. However, these conflicts can unravel even the closest of families. Peace returns when you step back and recognize the value of your teen establishing successful independence.

Think back and you may recall another time in your child's life when your authority was challenged, boundaries were pushed, and a lot of time was spent trying to test the limits of rules and regulations. The terrible 2s are but a preview of the tumultuous teen years.

Your child is going through an emotional time, but that doesn't mean you can't have perspective. You've been through this stage too, so humor can go a long way in making your child feel better about certain things. As long as you keep the lines of communication open, your child can feel comfortable and even feel OK to joke about it.

During this time, a once-sweet, complacent toddler begins to use his or her new language skills and budding sense of self to oppose any proposition. The word "No!" becomes a staple of communication. But this stage is simply a period of necessary self-discovery, a realization of individuality, and a frustration at being unable to express himself or herself fully because of a lack of verbal skills.

Despite episodes of foot stamping, indignant outbursts, and total self-absorption, children going through the terrible 2s remain endearing and adorable, while teens who ignore us, refuse to make eye contact, or, worse, roll their eyes are rarely, if ever, viewed as adorable.

By this point, the well-developed emotional bonds between parent and teen have become firmly cemented, allowing us to suspend much of our exasperation and exercise patience instead. Those tumultuous teenagers need love and guidance to successfully make it through these times.

Parents should let go of the feeling that teenage behavior has anything to do with them. This predictable, though explosive, period of human development represents the gateway to adulthood.

Helping Teens Navigate Puberty and Adolescence

Although your teenager's behavior does not represent a personal vendetta against you, it doesn't mean it should not be addressed. It is well known that parents who monitor their teen's behavior, set clear rules against drinking, and consistently enforce those rules help to reduce the likelihood of underage drinking. Therefore, you should brave the eye-rolling and sighing and be very clear about your expectations and concerns in a caring way.

Parents are supported by school programs that follow social influence models and include setting norms, addressing social pressures to drink, and teaching resistance skills. These programs are much more effective than past efforts that were simply scare tactics. These programs also offer interactive and developmentally appropriate information, including peer-led components.

Your teen has one foot in childhood and the other out the door to adulthood. His or her behavior is often erratic, being quite mature at times and, at other times, totally childlike. Many of the family's values may become a point of contention. It is difficult to reconcile that this child, the apple of your eye, can sometimes push back on family rules, is moody, or feels argumentative.

Make no mistake, teens still love and need their parents. The way in which they demonstrate this is counterintuitive but nonetheless true. Sometimes it is necessary to dig deeply to appreciate how much your child listens to what you have to say and needs your input and love. Sometimes you may have to take a leap of faith and remain confident that although your teen may behave on the surface as if he or she does not want to give you the time of day, he or she hears you. Your input is a critical piece in your teen's maturation.

As a parent, difficult as it may be at times, it can make a difference if you listen carefully without your agenda. Put down the smartphone and turn off the TV; offer your teen your undivided attention when the opportunity arises. When you demonstrate genuine interest without being distracted or displaying judgment, it can go a very long way in influencing the relationship that follows.

The Science Behind Adolescent Behavior

The risk-taking behavior that characterizes this period of adolescence is quite unnerving. For a long time, it was easy to assume that adolescents act out because of hormones. In fact, it appears that the risk-taking behavior may really be connected to changes in the regulation of neurotransmitters.

The Role of Neurotransmitters in Decision-making

Neurotransmitters, such as dopamine and serotonin, are chemicals in our bodies that are responsible for much of our behavior and emotions. Dopamine may be released in larger amounts in teens than it is in children or adults.

As a result of these neurotransmitters, adolescents may actually have a greater feeling of pleasure when they are excited than a child or an adult. Although it was believed years ago that adolescents lacked the maturity to reason through risky behavior effectively, we now see that both teens and adults probably reason through the pros and cons of risky behavior in a similar fashion. Teens and adults both play out in their mind what is great about an idea and what potentially might go wrong. The big difference lies in the payoff for adolescents when they do something that excites them; they have a greater dopamine response, which means greater pleasure. They don't reason through the pros and cons differently, but, rather, they justify their risky plan of action because they often cannot resist the huge pleasurable response that they can get.

Adult Versus Adolescent Dopamine-driven Decision-making

Imagine that an adult and a teen have the opportunity to attend a special party the night before an important day at work or school. Both will think about the importance of the next day. Both can conclude that going to a party may lead to staying out late. This, in turn, may result in a lack of proper sleep or the temptation to drink excessively, which could have negative consequences for the important event the next day.

The adult might conclude that the benefits of this party and temptation to drink are ill-timed and not worth the risk to his or her job and future. After all, there are always other parties. The teen will reason this out the same way, recognizing the possible outcomes of this decision, understanding that his or her future could be affected because of irresponsible actions.

The big divergence between the adult and the teen comes when the teen nevertheless chooses to go to the party. The driving force is the inability to resist the desire to experience the joy and excitement that come with attending a party with all of his or her friends.

A teen gets a much bigger emotional reward when the risky behavior pays off and thus is much more inclined to seek out and consider it worthwhile.

Brain Areas and Risk-taking

Other brain research is focused on separate areas of the brain and the way in which these regions interact and control adolescent reasoning. Two areas that play an important role in the adolescent brain are the prefrontal cortex and the amygdala.

The amygdala is a small, deep-seated area of the brain responsible for very immediate and instinctive emotional responses, such as fear and aggression. The prefrontal cortex is the area of the brain where higher reasoning takes place. This is an all-important area that controls much of the decision-making and planning, inhibits impulsive behavior, and balances risk-taking, social interaction, and self-awareness.

These areas mature at different rates. The amygdala becomes fully operational well before the prefrontal cortex, which continues to mature until approximately age 24 years. Neuroscientists believe that this difference between the more impulsive area of the brain, the amygdala, and the more rational area, the prefrontal cortex, plays an important role in adolescent behaviors, such as impulsive behaviors that seem to lack good decision-making regulation.

When a teen thinks, "I know I shouldn't text and drive, but I'll just do it this once because it will be so funny and I'm not able to pull over. Nothing will happen," it means the prefrontal cortex (the voice of reason) has not yet caught up with the amygdala (the instant gratification region).

The Importance of the Brain Remodeling Period

The increase in brain cell numbers peaks in adolescence and then goes through a time of remodeling or removing of brain cells. This process is called synaptic pruning and is influenced by the areas of the brain that the adolescent uses. It is a "use it or lose it" situation in the adolescent brain. Those connections that are frequently used are kept, while those with little value are removed. This synaptic pruning responds to the adolescent's environment and takes place in many regions of the brain, including the prefrontal cortex. It is very important that the teen has healthy habits during this critical period to ensure that the pruning that occurs is the best possible. Research has shown that exposure to drugs and alcohol during the teen years can change or delay these developments.

How to Cope With A Teen's Developing Brain

The science in the area of adolescent brain development is remarkable. Although we understand much more today than ever before about how the adolescent brain works, parents still struggle with trying to balance their concerns and the realization that they need to give their child space. It is ironic that teens, meanwhile, are annoyed with their parents and believe they exaggerate concerns.

It might be helpful to ask them "Are you capable of moving out to your own place and supporting yourself?" When they answer that they are not, you can tell them, "Well then, there is a price for everything in this world. Until you can support yourself, and while you are still living under my roof, these reasonable rules are the price you pay for accepting meals, transportation, and money." It might even help to explain that neurotransmitters and their developing brain are simply playing tricks on them that they can't yet see!

The Adolescent Stages

Adolescence has 3 emotional periods—early, middle, and late. We will focus heavily on the early period because this is the period that parents struggle with most. Once this phase has been successfully navigated, parents typically cruise more easily through the middle and late phases.

Early Adolescence

Behavior changes begin, on average, around age 11 years in girls and around age 12 years in boys. One reason is that the concrete thinking typical of younger children becomes more abstract. Preteens begin to recognize that some rules have a commonsense value (it makes sense to look both ways before crossing the street), whereas others are the family's values (this is the way we do it in our family). This opens the door to a new interpretation of rules for the preteen.

As a rejection of parental authority and wisdom occurs, especially in the oldest child, many parents are shocked, having never experienced any type of authority challenge before. It is not unusual for parents to grieve the loss of that younger child who now, in comparison, seemed to have been perfect.

Navigating This Tough Period

What are some guidelines that a parent can use to navigate this tough period?

- Remind yourself regularly that this stage, with its challenges, is an important period of development, and it allows your child to fully become himself or herself, apart from you.

- This is a period of questioning, determining the best way to get things done, and absolutely involves questioning your way.

- Most adolescents eventually come back to their family's values. But you will need to be patient.

- It's not personal.

- Remind yourself about your own specific teenage experience.

- Read lots of books about adolescence.

- Join a support group with other parents of preteens and teens.

- Try to spend more time asking open-ended questions that require more specifics about your child's day. Open-ended questions are those that require more than a simple "yes" or "no" answer. For instance, try to encourage dialogue with questions such as "What was the best part about today?" or "What was the most challenging part about today?" instead of simple closed-ended questions such as "Was school OK?"

- Be available. Let your child know that you are always willing to listen, and then really listen! Try to not jump to conclusions and give quick negative feedback; instead, try to elicit a course of action from your child by asking, "What do you think this situation calls for?" This is a wonderful way to validate that your child already knows the right thing to do, and, in turn, it is an opportunity for you to gain confidence in your child. If the answer disappoints you, it's still a terrific way to have a nonjudgmental, teachable moment.

Your child may not want to explicitly come to you and ask for help, so look for subtle cues and clues that he or she is seeking your input. When your child says something like, "I hate when we have to ask so-and-so to join us," he or she might be looking for ways to tell you more than what appears on the surface. Listen carefully.

Be sure to speak with your child about important issues such as

- Bullying

- Cyberbullying

- Texting and driving

- Drinking

- Drinking and driving

- Substance use

- Performance-enhancing substances

- Self-harm

Keeping the Channels of Communication Open

We know that preteens always do better when the channels of communication are open. Many people question the value of bringing up sensitive topics, particularly risk-taking behaviors such as unprotected sex, drug use, and alcohol consumption, because they believe that the mere discussion of those topics can plant ideas in a preteen's head. However, giving preteens a way to express themselves about difficult issues saves lives and does not encourage a preteen to do those very things.

Ask not just about your child but about your child's friends as well. After you have discussed a difficult topic such as alcohol use, continue with, "Well, what about your friends? Are they drinking?" Many preteens have a lot to say about their friends' risk-taking behaviors, even though the preteens themselves may not be participating. It can be quite eye-opening and offers a new opportunity to discuss the risks associated with having peers that engage in dangerous activities.

E-cigarette Use

E-cigarettes are exploding in popularity and are being used by both adolescents and adults. These devices—also called electronic nicotine delivery systems (ENDS)—are not a safe alternative to cigarette smoking.

E-cigarettes, ENDS, personal vaporizers, vape pens, e-cigars, e-hookahs, or vaping devices are products that produce an aerosolized mixture containing flavored liquids and nicotine that is inhaled by the user. Electronic nicotine delivery systems can resemble traditional tobacco products such as cigarettes, cigars, or pipes or common gadgets like flashlights, flash drives, or pens.

The American Academy of Pediatrics supports actions to prevent children and youth from using or being exposed to the vapor from ENDS (Figure 4-1).

Figure 4-1. E-cigarettes: A Threat to Health
Source: American Academy of Pediatrics Julius B. Richmond Center of Excellence

Asking the Difficult Questions

It is easy to think that your preteen is not going to engage in dangerous or unhealthy behaviors. Your picture of your child, after all, includes his or her toddler years and the sweet innocence of early childhood. You should, however, ask your preteen the tough questions in an open-ended, nonaccusatory way that is appropriate for preteens.

One way to do this is to say, "I've heard a lot in the news about vaping. What do you know about this?" Let your preteen tell you what he or she knows and then follow up with "Do you know anyone who vapes?" The conversation, once begun in an open, nonaccusing manner, clears the way for you to ask the final question, which is the one you are really interested in: "So have you tried it?"

It is always best to assume the position that you are simply curious not worried or, worse, in denial. Your relaxed behavior creates an open atmosphere that allows your preteen to be honest without worrying about hurting your feelings or worrying you.

If your preteen admits he or she has tried vaping, avoid reacting with anger, disgust, disappointment, or fear. The fact that preteens have tried vaping with their friends doesn't automatically mean that their health is in jeopardy or is considered an addiction. What is important is that your preteen was honest with you and told you about a potentially dangerous behavior. This gives you the opportunity to discuss the consequences of these behaviors with him or her to prevent a problem from developing. Stay calm. Tell your preteen how happy you are that he or she is sharing this with you and ask your preteen what his or her thoughts are about it. Why did he or she try it? Is he or she familiar with the effects of vaping? Show that you are listening to the answers. Be respectful of what your preteen tells you and then, in a calm and nonjudgmental manner, engage them in the facts about vaping. Give him or her material to read or recommend some online articles. The more your preteen knows about the effects and consequences, the better prepared he or she will be to say "no" if confronted with the same situation in the future. Vaping is not harmless and can result in nicotine addiction and other consequences. Talk to your preteen about safe alternative ways to enjoy himself or herself with friends.

Reporting Problem Behaviors Early for Guidance

Some parents are reluctant to talk about problems for fear it may reflect badly on them, or they mistakenly think it is just a phase. Professionals, however, are trained to assist with these very problems and prevent them from becoming larger problems. If your preteen admits to engaging in dangerous activities or if his or her friends are engaged in them, as a parent you should reach out to your preteen's pediatrician or other qualified health care professional for guidance on how to best address this. Trying to stay supportive and nonjudgmental as you guide your preteen greatly helps to build trust in your relationship.

Information to Share With Preteens and Teens

In conversations with teens, it is best to give them the information they need to make good decisions. Here are some facts that can help you discuss difficult issues with confidence.

Marijuana

Evidence clearly shows that marijuana is an addictive substance. Overall, 9% of those experimenting with marijuana will become addicted; this percentage increases to 17% among those who initiate marijuana use in adolescence and to a range of between 25% and 50% among teenagers who smoke marijuana daily.

A major study, published in 2012, in the *Proceedings of the National Academy of Sciences of the United States* also has shown that long-term marijuana use initiated in adolescence has negative effects on intellectual function and that the deficits in cognitive areas, such as executive function and processing speed, were not recovered by adulthood, even when cannabis use was discontinued.

Illicit Drug Use

The use of illegal drugs or the misuse of prescription medications or household substances is something many adolescents engage in occasionally, and a few do regularly. By the 12th grade, about half of adolescents have used an illicit drug at least once. The most commonly used drug is marijuana, but adolescents can find many substances, such as prescription medications, glues, and aerosols, in the home.

Alcohol

Each year, approximately 5,000 people younger than age 21 die as a result of underage drinking; this includes about 1,900 deaths from motor vehicle crashes, 1,600 as a result of homicides, 300 from suicide, as well as hundreds from other injuries such as falls, burns, and drownings. Many teens also do not realize that alcohol is one cause of cancer.

Alcohol and Brain Effects

Research conducted in which animals have been fed alcohol during this adolescent critical developmental stage continue to show long-lasting impairment from the alcohol as they age. It's simply not known how alcohol will affect the long-term memory and learning skills of people who began drinking heavily as adolescents.

Alcohol and Liver Effects

Elevated liver enzymes, indicating some degree of liver damage, have been found in some adolescents who drink alcohol. Young drinkers who have an unhealthy weight or have obesity are affected more than those of a healthy weight.

Middle Adolescence

Middle adolescence usually takes place during the high school years and is a time when your teenager is away from home more than he or she is at home, oftentimes spending an increased amount of time with friends. During this period, parents begin to feel ignored and neglected as opposed to the previous stage when they are challenged on everything. Your pediatrician can help you find the remarkable teenager living inside the "beast"!

Keziah's Story

Keziah was the poster child for a distracted, disengaged, borderline-rude, disinterested teen. She arrived at the doctor's office with her mother and a long list of symptoms that included headache, muscle aches and pains, problems with her period, and weight issues.

Keziah's father had passed away many years earlier, which had been a source of great trauma and stress for both Keziah and her mother. Keziah's mom did all the talking while Keziah remained engrossed in her magazine and did not make eye contact with the doctor. Keziah's mother talked about the multitude of problems that Keziah had and the many doctors that had been involved so far. The other doctors had given Keziah's mother many suggestions concerning her daughter's complaints, but they had little effect on Keziah's condition.

The doctor tried to engage Keziah, but she gave one-word answers. Her mother remarked that her daughter was often disengaged in exactly this fashion at home. She was baffled as to how to handle this.

The Doctor's Response

The doctor told Keziah's mom that, first of all, Keziah probably just needed some space. As she explained this, Keziah looked up from her magazine for the first time. The doctor told Keziah that she very much wanted to help her if, in fact, that was what she needed.

The doctor continued to explain that she understood that her mother loved her and was there to help her, but her mother had her own way of describing things that was not necessarily the way that Keziah might choose to describe things.

At that point, Keziah began to open up and discuss her feelings. Keziah needed to know that this discussion was about her complaints, not her mother's, and she became intensely interested when the doctor told her that she wanted and needed to hear about her issues directly from her. She gained confidence in speaking to the doctor when she saw that the doctor did not simply accept her mother's account of the problems but showed that her own story mattered. Keziah was frustrated and discouraged by her previous health care experiences and was protecting herself from further disappointment by being disengaged. Her rather typical, aloof teen behavior could easily be misinterpreted as disinterest. Pediatricians are trained to recognize typical teen behavior for what it is and what it is not. Keziah's behavior was off-putting, but she was hardly uninterested.

The Root of the Problem

Keziah, like most teens, had little patience for listening to her mom when she wasn't feeling well or in the mood for a discussion.

However, the doctor mentioned to Keziah that she might be asking a lot of her mom to always be a mind reader. How should Keziah's mother be expected to know when she should give her daughter some breathing room and when she should be there to help? Keziah recognized that this was a totally fair point.

Summary

There is a constant teen struggle to become independent, but it is a work in progress. Treating one's parent badly can be a teen's insensitive attempt to be assertive, a bad moment for hormones, or immaturity. There's a lot going on during middle adolescence!

Emotional Hallmarks of Middle Adolescence

Teens are moody, teens want what they want when they want it, but they also need love, understanding, and acceptance. Generally, as a rule, teens are very fair and just, but it might require some patience and creativity for their parents to be able to effectively point out to them, and get them to recognize, how their behavior looks from the adult perspective. Meeting teens on common ground, being genuinely engaged, and listening carefully can be a game changer. This allows the channels of communication to open and allows for common ground, which is always a good place to find compromise and solutions. When teens are not being challenged they can be wonderfully energizing, honest, optimistic, and socially conscientious.

Did You Know?

The percentage of teens in high school who drink and drive has decreased by more than half since 1991,* but more can be done to continue this trend. Nearly 1 million high school teens drank alcohol and got behind the wheel in 2011. Teen drivers are 3 times more likely than more experienced drivers to be involved in a fatal crash. Drinking any amount of alcohol greatly increases this risk for teens.

Research has shown that factors that help to keep teens safe include parental involvement, minimum legal drinking age and zero tolerance laws, and graduated driver licensing systems. These proven steps can protect the lives of more young drivers and everyone who shares the road with them.

*High school students aged 16 years and older who, when surveyed, said they had driven a vehicle one or more times during the past 30 days when they had been drinking alcohol.

Late Adolescence

Late adolescence occurs throughout the college years. This is a period when budding adults think about their futures and begin to plan their life strategies. If it hasn't already occurred, parents will now begin to see the light at the end of the tunnel. During this period, teens begin to be less contrary and more conversational. They are less defensive and more insightful. Parents often will see that family values are starting to reappear in their teen, who may even admit that there are aspects to their parents' advice that is appreciated. There will be a more direct effort to seek out their parents' opinion on important matters and decisions. You may see that certain responsibilities are handled without your prodding. Teens won't seem to get pleasure from testing their parents at every turn and may even say that they appreciate the effort that it takes to be a parent. They're getting there! Parents have been hearing for years, from friends, family, and professionals, that eventually the child they used to know will be back. In some families, this can mean they no longer have to endure the sharp tongue. In others, it may be a return to many of the family values that seemed to no longer matter; and in even others, it may amount to a renewed confidence that their teen can accept and conform to a responsible lifestyle. The day will come when parents once again are respected and valued. In late adolescence, parents begin to believe that this can come true.

Late Adolescence Tips for Parents

- See your teen as a person separate from yourself.

- Think about the purpose of this period. Your child is learning to be successfully independent.

- Know that there are no failures. A missed goal is another opportunity to learn and make adjustments and corrections.

- Believe that every learning experience is beneficial and protective for future successes.

- Find ways to be your teen's strongest advocate. Provide support where you can and guide with an open and nonjudgmental mind.

- Try to find common ground; look for opportunities to connect on these subjects.

- Listen, listen, listen.

- Remind yourself often about the purpose of this developmental period and lean on others for support.

- Have clear and firm rules and expectations.

- Enforce those standards firmly but in a kind and nonjudgmental manner.

- Try to spend time with your teen when he or she needs you. Remember, it may not be convenient for you.

- Model the behavior you want your teen to emulate.

- Be supportive but not a pal. Your child needs your parental expertise, not a buddy.

- Keep your own well-being in check. You need to be well mentally and physically to be at your best.

- Consider techniques such as the CBT adaptation of cognitive reconstructing detailed in this chapter.

- Say "I love you" in as many ways as you can.

Parents can't always be the good guy, and it isn't your job to be the friend. Over time, your kids will come to understand what you did, what you sacrificed, and what it means. And it will be worth every minute of it.

A Healthy Method of Coping with Adolescence

Some concepts of a specific type of behavioral therapy called cognitive behavioral therapy (CBT) can serve as a very healthy method of coping with adolescent behaviors that may push a parent's buttons.

Following are several core principles on which CBT is based:

1. Psychological problems are based, in part, on faulty or unhelpful ways of thinking—for example, a teen, Emma, is very attached to her best friend, but often questions their relationship stating, "I feel like Julie sometimes ignores me when other kids are around. Maybe she doesn't want to be as close with me as I want to be with her?"

2. Psychological problems are based, in part, on learned patterns of unhelpful behavior—Emma considers any expression of interest in other friends by her best friend as a threat to their relationship.

3. People with psychological problems can learn better ways of coping with them, thereby relieving their symptoms and becoming more effective in their lives—Emma can learn how to develop more self-confidence and objectively analyze the value of relationships. She can learn to recognize the objective signs that a relationship is close and genuine. She can confidently reassure herself and then conduct herself accordingly. She can learn how to successfully foster healthy, close friendships.

Strategies of CBT treatment usually involve efforts to change thinking patterns and include the following:

- Learning to recognize the problematic thinking that is creating problems
- Gaining a better understanding of the behavior and motivation of others
- Using problem-solving skills to cope with difficult situations
- Learning to develop a greater sense of confidence in one's own abilities

CBT is a tool that may be invaluable for parents who are trying to remain civil while interacting with their teens. Waiting until the situation is very difficult will only make the process more stressful. Any time is the right time to learn some advantageous coping techniques.

Using the Basics of CBT With Your Teen

Although you may not be able to change your teen's behavior, you certainly can change the way you handle that behavior. Instead of reacting, you can learn how to absorb the impact and redirect. With practice, the behavior will become less disturbing. Let's see what this looks like in practice by exploring the following steps:

1. Before saying a word, try to calm yourself by taking several deep and slow breaths.

2. Identify specifically what upsets you.

3. Analyze your mood now.

4. Identify automatic thoughts; what is popping into your head when your teen pushes those buttons?

5. Identify supportive objective evidence for those thoughts; what are the logical reasons to support those ideas that popped into your head?

6. Identify contradictory objective evidence for those thoughts; what are the logical reasons to reject the ideas that popped into your head?

7. Identify reasonable and balanced thoughts; analyze the logical evidence for and against the thoughts that popped into your head.

8. Analyze your mood now.

Putting It Into Practice

For example, let's consider this situation: Ms Smith is a single mom, raising her 16-year-old son, Jack, and her 11-year-old daughter, Ellie. Recently, she has become overwhelmed by the way that Jack speaks to her. Jack is a good student, with nice friends. He has always been very close to her, and they have had an open and honest relationship. However, now, Jack will abruptly tell his mom that he will be going out with his friends. When Ms Smith asks questions about his whereabouts, he says things like, "Gimme a break, Mom, I'm just hanging with my friends, I don't know where we'll be exactly, so leave me alone. Why do you need to know everything?"

Although Ms Smith is devastated on the inside, she hides it well. However, outwardly, she is furious that her son would speak to her this way and wants to know what she should do. She has tried to demand that he speak to her more respectfully, but that just escalates the friction between them. Jack will insist that he didn't do anything wrong. Ms Smith feels that her son, as she always knew him, is gone.

Does that strike a chord with anyone?

Approaching the Situation With the CBT Technique of Cognitive Reconstructing

1 **Try to regain control and calmness.** Ms Smith needs to think about what specifically is upsetting about Jack's behavior and try to remain calm. Taking several deep breaths can truly help to calm her for the moment. This is important because, to focus on the next steps, she will need to be present and focused.

2 **Identify what is specifically upsetting.** Jack is short tempered, rude, and borderline disrespectful.

3 **Analyze your mood.** Ms Smith needs to identify exactly how Jack's actions make her feel. They make Ms Smith feel angry, sad, humiliated, scared, and inadequate.

4 **Identify automatic thoughts.** Ms Smith states that she immediately thinks, "My son will have trouble with relationships in the future"; "I'm really not a good parent"; "I did this by marrying his father"; "I can't raise a son alone."

5 **Identify supportive objective evidence.** Ms Smith says that she knows that after a divorce, children in single family households have more issues surrounding emotional and mental health, including the risk of suicide, increased risk of school suspensions, and damage to the child's future competence. She also knows that teenagers typically go through a normal stage of being closer to their friends than to their parents.

6 **Identify contrary objective evidence.** Ms Smith admits that Jack has always been a good kid and continues, even now, to get good grades and have nice friends.

7 **Identify fair and balanced thoughts.** Ms Smith is able to think, "Jack really didn't say or do anything that was destructive or horrible. It was more the tone in his voice that was so disturbing and hurtful. I do ask a lot of questions, but that is my job as a parent. I really get caught up in things quickly and get ahead of myself. I can imagine that he possibly needs a little more space. Maybe I can approach this a bit differently with him."

8 **Analyze your mood now.** Ms Smith admits that she is now calmer and feels much better. She thinks that she might be able to address Jack in a less accusatory manner to get him to cooperate with her; she can also tell him about how she worries about him. She can have a more rational discussion with him about mutual respect. She can admit to him that it is difficult for her to have him grow up and not need her as much. She will try to stay calm when she speaks to him because she now recognizes that she has been reading a lot about herself into his behavior.

This process is one straightforward method of coping that has been adapted from CBT. With practice and patience, it is possible to maintain composure and have more meaningful discussions with a somewhat insensitive teen. When we respond well to conflicts, we help our teens by modeling appropriate behavior.

CHAPTER 5

Moodiness, Depression, and Anxiety: What Parents Need to Know

All teenagers face a chaotic mix of emotions, hormones, and ever-increasing expectations from school, parents, and friends. Parents may find it very difficult to determine whether their teenager's behavior is simply a typical response to the stresses of life or they are displaying the signs of a behavioral health issue that should be addressed by a professional.

A teen will typically grow out of moodiness, but depression usually does not go away on its own. Anxiety about school, sports, hobbies, or friends might dissipate as a teen learns to handle his or her busy schedule, but an anxiety *disorder* will not. Parents can reach out to their pediatrician to assist in addressing their teen's emotional concerns and figure out together what the proper action is, if any.

Moodiness

Moodiness is a regular part of adolescence. Typical teen behavior may include outbursts of emotion, erratic anger, staying up too late, and sleeping until noon. Teens may also act rather apathetic, lethargic, detached, isolated, or sometimes sad. Sometimes a teen will put on a set of headphones and play video games all day. Occasionally, a door may slam, or a crying fit may occur. You may feel that you don't know which teen you'll see on any given day—the "good" one or this "other" one.

If you notice that your teen's behavior regularly fluctuates, this is more consistent with moodiness and not a condition that would justify any treatment.

Teen Behavior: Explained With Science

Although brain growth may be finished by the time a child reaches school-age, its development and maturity are hardly complete. In fact, the brain is actually the last organ in the human body to mature. The size may no longer be changing, but the connections still are. The frontal lobes, the areas of the brain where executive function or decision-making, empathy, judgement, insight, and impulse control take place, is the last part to connect with the other parts. It is considered the control panel of the brain. We also know that when split-second decision-making is necessary, areas of the brain that control emotions, such as the limbic system and the amygdala, are maturing and responding faster than the frontal lobes. (See Chapter 4 for more on this topic.) This offers great insight into many aspects of typical teen behavior that commonly frustrate parents, such as impulsivity.

When a teen is faced with a snap decision, such as a dare to chug an alcoholic drink, the dare may win out because the emotional centers of the brain respond first, before the frontal lobes have had an opportunity to assist. Ten years later, when those connections are complete, a young adult may be less impulsive and might clearly consider the consequences of such an action.

How Does This Explain Adolescent Moodiness?

In the past, hormones were assumed to be the root cause of moodiness; however, we now believe moodiness is less about hormones and more the result of the imbalance between the frontal lobes and the limbic system. This imbalance may also increase a teen's response to stress. Excess stress during the teen years can alter the way in which the brain develops and create neurochemical imbalances that can influence depression. Feeling moody is a normal part of being a teenager. The following are some tips on how parents can handle this stage of adolescence:

- **Discuss the science with your teen.** Knowledge is power and arming your teen with information about the science behind brain development will help you both in understanding what is happening. It may help you to develop a better sense of empathy. Chances are your teen will be fascinated by this and will try to proactively control his or her reaction to things that he or she is sensitive about.

- **Stress the value of a healthy lifestyle.** Having a healthy lifestyle is the single most important thing that you and your family can do to promote good health, which also includes good mental health. You can help your teen understand his or her vulnerabilities and how having a healthy lifestyle can reduce and improve the ability to handle stress, lessen irritability, and improve moodiness. Encourage teens to consider the following topics:

  - Keep healthy sleep habits.
  - Eat a healthy and balanced diet.
  - Hydrate properly.
  - Stay active.
  - Maintain a balanced schedule for school responsibilities.
  - Encourage activities that teach mindfulness such as yoga, positive self-talk, controlled breathing, and muscle relaxation methods.

- **Share your insights from this time in your life.** A bit of humility can go a long way with your teen. When your teen gets moody, let him or her know that you had difficulties negotiating adolescence as well. Be relatable, be open, and be approachable.

- **Remember that mistakes are teachable moments.** All parents want to save their child from making mistakes, but errors in judgement and errors in life are opportunities to learn and grow. When children are terrified of making a mistake and disappointing their parents, it can lead to stress and moodiness. If your adolescent knows that you are someone that he or she can turn to without fear of looking weak or being considered a failure, it will be invaluable. A knee-jerk reaction by you to some of the things your teenager may share will only serve to alienate him or her and create a much moodier kid.

- **Encourage your teenager to discuss fears and concerns.** Brooding often occurs as a result of problems that an adolescent cannot solve alone. Let your teen tell you what those problems are and try to understand them from *your teen's* point of view.

- **Be a good listener and a nonjudgmental advisor.** Most people don't like to be lectured to, and teens particularly can't stand it. Hard as it might be, try to remain quiet and listen intently to your teen. When you truly listen, you may find that a lot more is shared. Your relationship will be stronger, and the moodiness will be less.

- **Ask permission to offer help, as opposed to telling your teen what to do.** Often, it's not what you say, but how you say it. Sometimes teens need to blow off steam and don't always want or need you to say anything. However, if you always have something to say, your teen might become more moody or want to avoid you. Try asking permission of your teen before voicing your thoughts. If he or she says, "No," as hard as it may be, just let it go for now. (If for some reason you don't feel that your teen is being honest with you, see the Depression section later in this chapter for more advice.)

- **Ask your teen about solutions.** Sometimes teens don't want to talk, because they want to solve a problem for themselves. They want you to listen, but not to advise. They want to discover and figure out what to do on their own. Try to guide your teenager to self-discovery and praise his or her ability to problem solve. It will be a great moment for you both.

- **Be ready to engage at any moment.** This is definitely a hard one. The moment your teen wants to talk may not come at a time that is best for you. Be prepared to set aside what you may be doing so you can give your full attention to your teen. These talks can include the most heartfelt, crucial bits and pieces of what is important to your adolescent. He or she is looking for your guidance. You need to be available when *he or she needs you* to build that strong relationship and bond that will go a long way to helping your adolescent control his or her emotions.

You should discuss with your pediatrician any time your child seems to have a negative mood for longer than 2 weeks. At any time that you simply feel something just isn't right about your teen, trust your gut and have a talk with your doctor. It is always better to be on the safe side of these behavioral health issues.

Depression

Symptoms of depression include many of the same symptoms as moodiness: irritability, sadness, fatigue, and sleep issues. The distinction is when these symptoms persist for longer than a 2-week period. Teen depression isn't a weakness or something that can be overcome with willpower—it can have serious consequences and require long-term treatment. For most teens, depression symptoms will get better with treatment. This may include psychological counseling, medication, or both.

Knowing the signs of depression will help you put your teen's moodiness in a better perspective. Moodiness gets its definition from the fact that the behavior regularly fluctuates. A distinguishing factor for depression is the persistence of the depressed mood and the abrupt change in behavior. Depression can seem to have started out of the blue.

The Causes of Depression

Depression is not simply a matter of poor mood. It is a serious medical condition, one that affects the way a person feels, thinks, and behaves. There are several contributing factors that we need to recognize.

- **Neurotransmitters.** Neurotransmitters are chemicals in our brain that carry signals to other parts of the brain. A specific balance of neurotransmitters must exist for our emotions and behavior to function in a healthy way. When this balance is altered because chemicals are abnormal or not working correctly, it can lead to depression.

- **Hormones.** We know that before puberty begins, the rate of depression is equal for boys and girls, but once puberty begins, the rate of depression becomes nearly twice as common for girls. The changes in the body's balance of hormones may play a role in causing or triggering depression.

- **Genetics.** Depression tends to run in families and is more common in blood relatives who have the condition.

- **Adverse childhood experiences (ACEs).** Adverse childhood experiences, such as physical or emotional abuse, loss of a parent, divorce, poverty, or other difficult situations, may cause changes in the brain that make a person more susceptible to depression.

- **Learned patterns of negative thinking.** Teen depression may be linked with learning to feel helpless, rather than developing a sense of confidence for coping with life's challenges. Parents can benefit by trying to understand their own patterns of behavior in the family. Sometimes our own behavior patterns are not consistent with what is needed to support good emotional health. For example, not allowing your teenager to take responsibility for his or her own actions (eg, schoolwork) or needs (preparing lunches, cleaning clothes, chores) can lead to a lack of confidence in adolescents.

Recognizing Depression

Although depression is fairly common, a stigma exists around the diagnosis of any type of behavioral health condition. In 2015, an estimated

3 million adolescents aged 12 to 17 years in the United States had at least one major depressive episode in the past year. This number represented 12.5% of the US population of children aged 12 to 17. Untreated depression likely won't get better on its own and may worsen or lead to other problems. Depressed teenagers may be at risk of suicide, even if signs and symptoms don't appear to be severe. Knowing what to look for can help you to recognize if your teen needs help.

Signs of Depression

- **Having trouble falling or staying asleep or sleeping too much.** This may sound like every typical teenager, but the following are some distinctions:

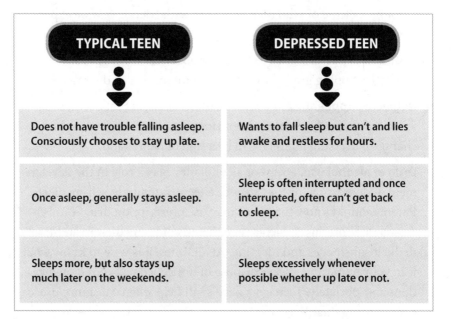

TYPICAL TEEN	DEPRESSED TEEN
Does not have trouble falling asleep. Consciously chooses to stay up late.	Wants to fall sleep but can't and lies awake and restless for hours.
Once asleep, generally stays asleep.	Sleep is often interrupted and once interrupted, often can't get back to sleep.
Sleeps more, but also stays up much later on the weekends.	Sleeps excessively whenever possible whether up late or not.

- **Feeling tired or having little energy.** This is independent of sleep. Even with good sleep there is tiredness and little energy.

- **Poor appetite or overeating.** Eating behaviors that have changed abruptly with a very poor appetite, obvious weight loss, or gross overeating may become obvious. Developing or having an eating disorder is also possible with depression.

- **Moving or speaking extremely slowly.** Your teen's speech is unusually and painfully slow.

- **Excessive fidgeting or restlessness.** Teens who seem unable to stay still and who move and pace restlessly may be depressed.

- **Frequent complaints of unexplained body aches and headaches, which may include frequent visits to the school nurse.** Teens may have endless complaints of many different types of aches and pains. Depression is considered and further discussed, particularly for those teens who are tested for a physical cause of the pain but whose test results prove to be typical.

- **Social isolation.** Teens who stay locked in their rooms for inordinate amounts of time or who don't hang out with friends may be experiencing depression.

- **Poor school performance or frequent absences from school.** Abruptly slipping grades are an important marker of depression.

- **Neglected appearance.** Behavior pattern changes that occur, such as lack of showering, little concern for proper hygiene, or an abrupt change in dressing manner, can be a sign of depression.

- **Drug or alcohol use.** Drugs or alcohol may play a role in the development of depression, or they may be a teen's attempt to self-medicate. Parents should know that teens may use prescription drugs or over-the-counter products, such as cough and cold remedies, in addition to illicit substances and nicotine. At all times, it is wise to know what is in your home and always dispose of unneeded or expired medications appropriately. Teenagers need swift help when substance use is complicating their lives.

- **Angry outbursts, disruptive or risky behavior, and other acting-out behaviors.** When a teen starts to act out with unpleasant, out of the ordinary behaviors, it could be a warning sign to consider the cause behind the behaviors.

- **Self-harm (eg, cutting or burning).** Behaviors that include self-harm such as cutting or burning, are red flags for depression. Some explanations for self-harm include feeling empty inside, feeling over or under stimulated, being unable to express feelings, loneliness, feelings that are misunderstood by others, being fearful of intimate relationships, and worry over increasing responsibilities. Self-harm is generally a coping mechanism to relieve painful or hard-to-express feelings and is not a suicide attempt. The relief is temporary, and without treatment this can become a self-destructive cycle. Self-mutilation can also serve as a way to have control over one's body when it seems like nothing else in life can be controlled. Often teens who cut themselves also can have an eating disorder. (See Chapter 2 for more on eating disorders). Teens engaged in behaviors such as this will try to hide their wounds. Wearing long-sleeved clothing all year round may be a tip-off that something is wrong.

Screening Tools for Depression

There are different screening tools for detecting depression. The screening tool that pediatricians often use is the Patient Health Questionnaire-9 (PHQ-9) (Figure 5-1), which provides a score that correlates with the severity of depression. Simple counseling might be recommended for a low rating, whereas a higher rating might necessitate a referral to a therapist and medication management.

The screening tool uncovers negative and potentially dangerous thoughts and feelings that may be hidden from everyone.

PATIENT HEALTH QUESTIONNAIRE-9 (PHQ-9)

Over the last 2 weeks, how often have you been bothered by any of the following problems? (Use "✔" to indicate your answer)	Not at all	Several days	More than half the days	Nearly every day
1. Little interest or pleasure in doing things	0	1	2	3
2. Feeling down, depressed, or hopeless	0	1	2	3
3. Trouble falling or staying asleep, or sleeping too much	0	1	2	3
4. Feeling tired or having little energy	0	1	2	3
5. Poor appetite or overeating	0	1	2	3
6. Feeling bad about yourself — or that you are a failure or have let yourself or your family down	0	1	2	3
7. Trouble concentrating on things, such as reading the newspaper or watching television	0	1	2	3
8. Moving or speaking so slowly that other people could have noticed? Or the opposite — being so fidgety or restless that you have been moving around a lot more than usual	0	1	2	3
9. Thoughts that you would be better off dead or of hurting yourself in some way	0	1	2	3

FOR OFFICE CODING ___0___ + _____ + _____ + _____

=Total Score: _____

If you checked off any problems, how difficult have these problems made it for you to do your work, take care of things at home, or get along with other people?

Not difficult at all	Somewhat difficult	Very difficult	Extremely difficult
☐	☐	☐	☐

Figure 5.1. Patient Health Questionnaire-9

Source: Developed by Drs. Robert L. Spitzer, Janet B.W. Williams, Kurt Kroenke and colleagues; http://www.phqscreeners.com/sites/g/files/g10016261/f/201412/PHQ-9_English.pdf.

The answers to the PHQ-9 when scored reveal the degree of depression severity. It identifies whether an emergency exists or if a more relaxed approach is appropriate. Once a diagnosis of depression is made, this tool can be used to monitor the progress of the illness as well. Levels of depression are as follows:

- A score of 0–4 correlates with *None–minimal depression.*

- A score of 5–9 correlates with *Mild depression.*

- A score of 10–14 correlates with *Moderate depression.*

- A score of 15–19 correlates with *Moderately severe depression.*

- A score of 20–27 correlates with *Severe depression.*

However, any time children indicate that they have or have had thoughts that they might be better off dead or hurting themselves in some way, an immediate referral is made regardless of the total score.

Treating Depression

If your teen has been diagnosed with depression, it will be categorized as minimal, mild, moderate, moderately severe, or severe. This will help to determine what treatment option will be most effective. For less significant depression, counseling is the first line of treatment. There are different forms of therapy, of which cognitive behavioral therapy (CBT) is one of the most popular. (There is more detail on CBT in Chapter 4). If depression is more significant, antidepressant medication will be prescribed, usually in conjunction with counseling. The medications used most often are called selective serotonin reuptake inhibitors or SSRIs. They work by altering the balance of the neurotransmitter serotonin in the brain. Treatment for depression is effective and can restore happiness and quality of life for your teen. Fear and worry should never come from taking action, but from the consequences of inaction.

Talking With Your Teen About Depression

Sometimes a depressed teen doesn't have outward noticeable behavior changes, but rather more negative and destructive thoughts and feelings. Unless your teen is honest and open about these destructive thoughts and feelings, you may not be aware that they exist. The following is a list of common destructive feelings and strategies on how to have a more meaningful dialogue with your teen:

- **Having a loss of interest or pleasure in regular everyday activities.** If your teen suddenly starts spending a lot of time in his or her room and seems to have lost interest in the things that have previously caused happiness, don't chalk it up to "typical teenage brooding"; instead, make a point of being available. Let your teen know that you are concerned, and that you are there and willing to talk, even if it means waking you in the middle of the night or calling you at work. Let your teenager know that you will always be there.

- **Having a loss of interest in family and friends.** Likewise, if your teen used to join everyone for dinner and now clearly avoids family or friends, make a point of having a discussion about it. Don't ever conclude that bringing up a behavior will somehow make things worse. It won't. Again, always make a point of making your availability known.

- **Feelings of sadness, which may include bouts of unexplained crying.** Parents know that there is a lot of drama that goes along with being a teenager, but don't ignore bouts of unexplained crying and sadness. Your teen may need space to move forward with a challenge; however, if you don't offer any support, how would he or she know that you are there? There is no substitute for saying that you want and are able to help.

- **Feelings of hopelessness or just feeling empty.** Be on the lookout for remarks such as "I'll never be able to do that" or "Things will never be like that for me." Note how often they are made. They may be your only window into how your teen is feeling on the inside.

- **Low self-esteem.** Teens who experience low self-esteem are at a great risk for depression. See Chapter 2 for an in-depth discussion and ways to address self-esteem and body image with your teen.

- **Trouble concentrating, such as in reading or completing homework.** Depression may be present any time that competency in schoolwork abruptly changes. Your teen may not even know that he or she is depressed but may recognize and admit that he or she is having a difficult time with concentration. Seek help if this is the case. Children who have attention-deficit/hyperactivity disorder (ADHD) can be at a higher risk for depression.

- **Feelings of worthlessness or guilt, feeling that the family has somehow been let down.** This may be another area where you may only hear a fleeting comment that suggests a teenager feels this way. Never ignore those comments. It is better to make a fuss about nothing, than to ignore something that potentially could be life changing.

- **Having exaggerated self-blame, being very self-critical, fixating and dwelling over past failures.** Parenting is not easy and by the time your child reaches puberty, it is more challenging. Help your teenager to understand that there really are no failures in this world, as long as we always learn from our mistakes. Help your teen to be kind to himself or herself; puberty and adolescence are times of great change and immense growth. Be confident and optimistic for the future. Be your teen's greatest fan and seek help if you don't see improvement with this attitude.

- **Having extreme sensitivity to rejection or failure and seeking excessive reassurance.** With some teens it can seem impossible to give all of the reassurance necessary to make them comfortable. When you feel that you can never seem to say or do enough to help your teen, it is wise to ask for help.

- **Thinking that being dead would be good and the world would be better off without your teen.** This is always a situation that requires immediate help.

Who Is at Risk for Depression?

Many underlying factors can increase the risk of developing or triggering teen depression. Here are things that we know to look out for.

- Living with issues that challenge high self-esteem, such as having obesity, difficulty with peers, long-term bullying, or academic difficulties.

- Having witnessed or been the victim or perpetrator of violent acts such as physical or sexual abuse.

- Having other behavior health conditions, such as bipolar disorder, anxiety disorders, personality disorders, anorexia, or bulimia.

- Being gay, lesbian, bisexual, or transgender in an unsupportive environment.

- School challenges such as having a learning disability or ADHD.

- Living with a chronic physical illness such as cancer, diabetes, or asthma, or regular chronic pain.

- Having any physical disability.

- Having certain personality traits, such as low self-esteem or being overly dependent, self-critical, or pessimistic.

- Having a problem with alcohol, nicotine, or other drugs.

- Having a parent, grandparent, or other blood relative with depression, bipolar disorder or alcoholism. Knowing that your family is in a high-risk category makes having discussions about depression and other behavioral health disorders important. Keeping the channels of communication open about this is a big step toward ensuring everyone is happy and safe.

- Having a family member or friend who committed suicide. Studies show that a considerable number of youth suicides and suicide attempts occur in the wake of the self-inflicted death or injury of someone else. Having discussions together allows you to talk about the ways in which a person who is having difficulty can get help and support.

- Having a family life that is filled with conflict. Families that are under such stresses on an everyday basis are at risk.

- Having experienced recent stressful life events, such as parental divorce, parental military service, or the death of a loved one.

Anxiety

Having anxiety about stresses in life is typical and different than having an anxiety disorder. Everyone experiences anxiety or nervousness. Often the type of anxiety that affects us in everyday life has benefits. A teen might be anxious about an upcoming exam, but this serves to encourage him or her to study until certain that he or she knows the material. A teen may worry about starting driving lessons and become very jittery at the thought of getting behind the wheel, especially for the first time. This differs from an actual anxiety disorder that requires treatment.

A parent can help teens with anxiety in many ways. Many of these tips may seem trivial when considered individually, but when considered as a whole, they can reduce and help control the effects of normal anxiety.

Redirect—Sometimes when teens are anxious, they may want to avoid contact with the stressful situation and choose to stay at home, alone with their thoughts. However, this can lead to thinking endlessly about whatever is bothering them. Often the best way to get rid of anxiety is to simply get out and be distracted by something more pleasant. You can help redirect your teen by arranging or suggesting a pleasurable outing.

Eat Well—There is no escaping the fact that eating well makes you feel better, and certain foods, such as caffeine, can make anxiety worse. Many teens drink too many caffeinated beverages, and this alone can make them very jittery.

Avoid Anxiety-Provoking Stimuli—Teens and parents may not fully realize the impact of certain situations that can be avoidable. If your teen has nightmares after scary movies, then he or she should avoid watching that type of movie. As a parent, if you know of any situations that often cause your teen anxiety, it may be helpful to chat about this with your teen and bring any strong concerns about this to his or her pediatrician.

Be Active—During physical activity, chemicals that make us feel good, called endorphins, are released, as well as hormones that are connected to reducing stress. Teens should aim for at least 60 minutes of moderate to vigorous activity daily or nearly daily to maintain health and reduce stress.

Mindfulness and Yoga—Practicing meditation, mindfulness, or yoga have been shown to improve a person's well-being and reduce anxiety. It is possible to learn and practice techniques to control breathing, thoughts, and biologic stress responses and improve the awareness of the body's response to stressful situations; all of these techniques help to control stress and anxiety.

Positive Thinking—Although they may sound silly at first, positive thinking techniques can be very helpful. The negative thoughts that often accompany anxiety are replaced by positive, confident self-talk. What begins as an exercise can become a constructive coping mechanism. Some teens may benefit from writing positive thoughts in a journal, while others may need to engage in thought-stopping (see Thought Stopping text box).

Friends—Parents can help their teens consider the importance in choosing friends who are supportive and genuine and have good values.

Thought Stopping

Negative thoughts are an upsetting part of anxiety. Sometimes children with negative thoughts find it hard to think about anything else or even to fall asleep when negative thoughts and worries get started. Thought stopping is a way to end negative thoughts before they interfere with daily life.

To stop unpleasant thoughts

- Say or yell "STOP" out loud (or in your mind if you are not alone).
- Imagine a stop sign or big red letters that spell STOP.
- Breathe in.
- When you breathe out, say "I'm OK" (or "I'm safe" or "All is well").
- Picture your safe place if you have one (or a peaceful scene, if not).
- Repeat these steps until the negative thoughts are replaced by the positive ones.

Thought stopping steps should be done as soon as an unpleasant thought or worry comes up. The longer your child waits to stop negative thoughts, the harder it is to stop them.

Source: American Academy of Pediatrics. *Understanding Anxiety Disorders in Children.* Itasca, IL: American Academy of Pediatrics. In press

Anxiety Disorders

An anxiety disorder can be overwhelming and even terrifying. Nearly 1 out of 7 children and teens develop an anxiety disorder, which is the most common mental health condition among all age groups. Some symptoms may be less intense than others, even though they may appear relentless to the teen. An anxious teen may experience guilt, fear, or even irritability. Often the cause of the anxiety is unclear. Anxiety is not a periodic problem but one that causes problems in everyday activities. This is often referred to as functional impairment. Anxiety disorders can be more difficult to recognize than other behavioral disorders because the symptoms are often invisible; symptoms exist as part of the teen's emotions and thoughts and not as outward behaviors. Only when the symptoms are expressed in actual behavior, such as weight loss, sleeplessness, or refusal to attend school, will it attract the attention needed for the parent to consider seeking help.

Anxiety Can Look Like a Physical Illness

I saw a teenage girl in the office who told me she had lightheadedness and heart palpitations that occurred mostly when she got up from lying down. She stated that she often needed to stay home because the feeling of lightheadedness made her feel like she might faint, and she was scared to feel this way in school. When she needed to stay home, she often missed up to a week of school.

She was growing well, had friends, and was a good student. Her diet was a healthy one and she had decent sleep habits when she was feeling OK. When she was dealing with this problem, her sleep patterns were sometimes affected, mostly because she would sleep a great deal during the daytime while at home. In all other ways she did not feel ill at all.

She was referred to a cardiologist and a neurologist to rule out any serious problems with those areas that could account for her complaints. She had blood testing as well. All of her results were normal, but she was still experiencing symptoms and still occasionally missing school.

This is the point at which I met her. I discussed with her and her mother all the past history. Given the test results, I knew it was unlikely that there was a serious physical illness. There was reason to assume that she might have something called postural hypotension, which can cause a person to feel very light-headed when sitting or standing up too quickly. It does not have any medical significance, but it can feel scary.

Anxiety Can Look Like a Physical Illness (continued)

Once you know that you have it, taking more time to let your body acclimate to sitting or standing before rushing off can prevent the uncomfortable sensations. Often once a problem is understood to be harmless, it relieves a major anxiety that people have wondering what is wrong with them.

My patient looked very relieved as we talked about this. I next asked her the most important question concerning her problem. I asked her if she believes that she worries a lot? She smiled and said, "Absolutely." I explained to her that any 2 people could have postural hypotension and feel weird when getting up. However, those with an anxiety disorder who experience a postural hypotension episode may become quite panic stricken and worry endlessly. This reaction is opposite to that of individuals with no anxiety condition who might be a bit concerned if an episode occurs but do not continuously stress about the uncomfortable sensation once it has passed.

I mentioned that people with anxiety disorders can spend large amounts of time worrying about all sorts of things, many of which are not at all likely to happen, such as being in an airplane crash or being inside the house during a storm when a tree crashes through the roof. She looked astonished and told me that she worried about both of these things regularly.

She admitted to me that she had considered the connection between her physical symptoms of lightheadedness and palpitations with other things that caused her anxiety, but she couldn't tell by herself if this was an accurate connection. She and her mother decided that she should see a therapist for her anxiety.

Types of Anxiety Disorders

The types of anxiety disorders vary, and each has its own nuances. Table 5-1 includes a list of the most common anxiety disorders in teens and a brief description and summary of a typical treatment plan, keeping in mind that care is always individualized for every person.

Table 5-1. Types of Anxiety Disorders and Treatments

Name	Description	Treatment
Generalized Anxiety Disorder (GAD)	Characterized by excessive anxiety and worry about a number of events or activities with the intensity, duration, or frequency of the anxiety out of proportion to the likelihood of the event. The teen finds it difficult to control the worrying. There are also associated physical symptoms such as chest pain, headache, restlessness, being on edge, fatigue, sleep disturbances, irritability, and more.	First-line therapy is usually a behavioral intervention such as cognitive behavioral therapy (CBT). In CBT, a person learns methods to cope with and control their anxiety. When necessary, medication can be added to the treatment plan, often a selective serotonin reuptake inhibitor (SSRI). Other behavioral therapies include • Biofeedback (the power to use your thoughts to control your body and its involuntary functions, often to improve a health condition such as migraines or chronic pain.) • Stress management • Specific therapeutic programs for teens

Obsessive Compulsive Disorder (OCD)	This is a complex disorder that is characterized by **obsessions,** which are recurrent, persistent, intrusive thoughts that are not about real-life problems, but cause an individual significant anxiety and distress.
	
	Individuals try to ignore the obsessions because they recognize they are products of their own mind.
	
	Compulsions are repetitive behaviors to which a person is driven to prevent or relieve distress. The person usually recognizes that these compulsions are unreasonable.
		• CBT is used most commonly.
		• Medication, generally an SSRI, often is used in conjunction.
		• Social support systems
		  – School to assist with coping
		  – Community with peer groups or family groups
		• Techniques to decrease arousal of OCD
		  – Biofeedback
		  – Mindfulness
		  – Deep muscle relaxation
		  – Meditation
		• Keeping a regular routine and maintaining a healthy lifestyle.

Post-traumatic Stress Disorder (PTSD)	PTSD consists of a set of symptoms, such as jitteriness, flashbacks, nightmares, or a persistent sense of fear, that develop in response to a major traumatic event. In addition, sleeping problems, trouble concentrating, feelings of detachment, irritability, aggression, or loss of interest can occur. The person may continuously relive the event or purposefully avoid reminders of the event.	A behavioral intervention such as CBT often is used in conjunction with a medication like an SSRI.

Table 5-1. Types of Anxiety Disorders and Treatments (*continued*)

Name	Description	Treatment

Phobias	Characterized by intense and irrational fears of specific things or situations such as heights, flying, or animals.
	
	A person with a phobia will avoid feared things and situations.
	• Physical symptoms of anxiety, such as nausea, trembling, or sweating, occur.
		• CBT is used most commonly.
		• Medication when necessary.
		• Social support systems
		  – School to assist with coping
		  – Community with peer groups or family groups
		• Techniques to decrease arousal
		  – Biofeedback
		  – Mindfulness
		  – Deep muscle relaxation
		  – Meditation
		• Keeping a regular routine and maintaining a healthy lifestyle.

Social Phobias	Social phobias are characterized by intense fear of social situations or speaking in front of others with avoidance of eye contact or interaction with others as well as excessive worry about the thoughts and opinions of others.	• CBT is used most commonly.
		• Medication is used in conjunction when necessary.
		• Social support systems
		  – School to assist with coping
		  – Community with peer groups or family groups
		• Techniques to decrease arousal
		  – Biofeedback
		  – Mindfulness
		  – Deep muscle relaxation
		  – Meditation
		• Keeping a regular routine and maintaining a healthy lifestyle.

Panic Attacks	Panic attacks come on suddenly with intense fearfulness. The person has an overwhelming fear of dying or losing control, with physical symptoms such as dizziness, shortness of breath, and racing heartbeat.	• CBT is used most commonly.
		• Short-term course of medication, usually a benzodiazepine, when necessary.
		• Social support systems
		  – School to assist with coping
		  – Community with peer groups or family groups
		• Techniques to decrease arousal
		  – Biofeedback
		  – Mindfulness
		  – Deep muscle relaxation
		  – Meditation
		• Keeping a regular routine and maintaining a healthy lifestyle.

Taking to Your Teen About Anxiety

Many parents simply don't bring up their concerns about anxiety with their teen or their pediatrician for fear that talking about anxiety will create a problem or because they think it is just part of their teen's personality. However, anxiety disorders that go untreated may eventually lead to poor school performance, an inability to maintain friendships, or depression.

Many teens suffer in silence because of fears such as

- Something is wrong with their mind

- They are the only one with this problem

- It is embarrassing, especially for teens with OCD

- Their friends won't understand, will judge them, or will think less of them.

To ensure that your teen receives the help that he or she needs, talk with your pediatrician. Here are some important questions to ask yourself or your teen. Does your teen

- **Excessively worry about things that seem unreasonable or irrational?** *"It seems to me that many things worry you. Do you think that is true?"*

- **Have difficulty controlling worrying?** *"When you start to worry, do you have a hard time controlling it?"*

- **Have restlessness, trouble concentrating, aches and pains, trouble sleeping, or fatigue?** *"Have you noticed any type of connection between having a lot of worries during the day and some of these other problems that have started, such as your aches and pains?"*

- **Have anxiety problems that affect academics, social relationships, or daily activities?** *"With all this worrying it seems like your school work is suffering and maybe you're not able to enjoy your friends. Do you feel like that?"*

- **Have an underlying problem that would explain all the worrying?** *"Is there anything going on with you or in our family that is bothering you?"*

- **Have anxiety problems that occur on most days?** *"How often do you feel these concerns or worries?"*

- **Have a history of worrying a great deal? Did your teen have trouble separating from you as a child, have lots of fears, or experience lots of stress?** *"You know, you were always a child who worried. When you were little you never wanted to go for a sleepover and you had lots of fears about all kinds of stuff. Do you remember being like that?"* Or you might ask, *"Do you think that you have always been a worrier?"*

- **Have a family member who has anxiety problems?** *"I think you know that I also have a problem with worrying, so it's OK that you do too. We need to see your pediatrician and get you some help. Tons of kids feel the same way. You can feel better. Let's take care of this together."*

Modeling Healthy Behavior

Parents should model the behavior that they expect from their teen. When your teen has an anxiety disorder, it becomes that much more important that you model the type of behavior that will help your child or teen learn how to cope more effectively with stress.

Consider the following examples and how you would respond:

You are running errands with your teen and you get a phone call that an event your other child is attending was canceled, and you must come and pick up your other child immediately. How do you respond in front of your teen? Do you calmly explain that you need to quickly change plans, or do you get flustered and upset?

You get an email from your boss late Friday night telling you to complete a project by Monday. You had a full weekend of activities planned. Do you have a meltdown in front of your teen? Do you get agitated and act stressed out all weekend or do you calmly plan out your strategy to accomplish your revised goals?

The news is full of sad and stressful occurrences. Are you affected by this? Do you talk in front of your teen about how frightened you are to go to a mall or an airport, or to walk around the neighborhood?

Life is stressful and there are elements to our world that are frightening, and how you react to these stresses and elements can have a huge effect on your teen. It pays to ask yourself whether your own daily behavior is a help or a hindrance. Consider discussing this with your child's therapist or pediatrician and asking for guidance.

Good Mental Health

Knowing when to ask for help is one of the most important and difficult parts of parenting. When it comes to mental health, the only thing a family should legitimately fear is not seeking help when it is needed. There is help for these disorders and it's important to make sure you know the signs and take steps to make sure your child or teen is happy and healthy.

CHAPTER 6

The Value of Your Child's One-on-one Time With the Pediatrician

The role of the pediatrician in your child's health care has evolved to include much more than diagnosing strep throat and administering the required childhood immunizations. Today, your pediatrician is a highly trained child specialist who can advise you and your family about all aspects of growth, development, overall health, and wellness.

Achieving this holistic outcome for children and teens and, in particular, supporting parents through puberty entails education and advice about the following:

- The physical aspects of growth and development
- The emotional aspects of growth and development
- The aspects of health and wellness that are important to both

The Benefit to Alone Time

Your child should see the doctor once a year. Birthdays are a good time to remind yourself of the need for a well-child visit (also known as a *health supervision visit*). When a child is approaching puberty, most pediatricians will let parents know that at one of the next well visits it will be time to spend some portion alone with their child. Typically, though, this does not begin prior to age 12 and is modified to fit the developmental aspects for each child. Parents have a somewhat predictable array of reactions and responses, including the following:

- "Is it that time already?"
- "I don't think my child will like that."
- "Isn't he [or she] too young?"
- "Will you be sharing this private and important information with me?"
- "Would you like me to leave the room now?"
- "Why exactly do you need to do this?"

Before directly addressing these responses, let's first talk about how an adolescent office visit typically goes.

The Adolescent Office Visit

Although pediatricians lend their own style to their examinations, many begin by starting the visit with the adolescent and parents together. The doctor asks the typical questions, covering the past year's medical history; reviewing any past and current problems; discussing medications or complimentary alternative medications that are used; reviewing allergies and eating, sleeping, and elimination habits; discussing social history, which includes family, school, and peer dynamics; among other topics. This part of the visit is directed primarily to the parent, though the adolescent is always able to chime in as necessary. Before the physical examination, the doctor will ask the parent to allow some time alone with the adolescent.

Sometimes parents who know what is coming will ask several times, "Should I go now?" while we all chat together. It is fine to ask the doctor to let you know when it is appropriate to leave so that you can feel comfortable with the process.

Parents and adolescents should understand the broad rationale behind this routine. The pediatrician has built a relationship with you and your budding adolescent, sometimes over the entire course of your adolescent's lifetime, sometimes over a shorter period. No matter the amount of time, all patient/doctor relationships are built on mutual trust and respect. The goals of the pediatric health care relationship include guiding and protecting the health and well-being of your adolescent, but also preparing your adolescent for navigating an adult health care experience. In this way, we bridge this gap together and pave the way for your adolescent to confidently and independently join the adult health care world.

In many families, the biggest challenge is not how much *more* parents can do for their kids but how they can effectively do *less*. Parents should know that they can allow their adolescents to try, to fail, to learn, and to grow. We need to teach and prepare adolescents for the independence and responsibilities that lie ahead in both the health care arena and life in general. Parents and pediatricians can partner in this effort to help kids and teens stand successfully on their own two feet.

Addressing Parental Reactions

Here are some of the questions that parents generally ask when told that the doctor needs to spend some of the time alone with their adolescent.

"Is it that time already?"

The answer is…not really. The goal, however, is to begin to forge a more adultlike relationship with your child before adolescence is in full swing. With most families, the doctor/patient relationship has focused primarily on the parent and pediatrician. And certainly, through the early years, this was completely appropriate. However, when you consider that one goal of parenthood is to prepare children to become adept and independent, teens need to begin to embrace and accept responsibility for their own health care. One reason for beginning this transition a little early is to foster that sense of responsibility and confidence in adolescents for taking charge of their own health. Many kids need a lot of time to do this. Often when a doctor asks children direct questions with their parents in the room, such as what they ate for breakfast, when their last period was, and how they did in school this semester, they inevitably turn to their parent for answers! By starting the process a little early, kids might have a better chance of being more self-reliant and comfortable when they really need to answer tougher questions.

"I don't think my child will like that."

When parents say that they don't think that their child will be pleased about them having to leave the room, it is often a good sign that this is the very thing the child needs most. Children need to develop an ability to think independently, behave responsibly, relate to adults, and carry on a conversation with an adult. If this is going to be very difficult, that by itself implies that we need to build some skill sets. Pediatricians are, in fact, not your physician but your child's. Pediatricians have been trained to recognize signs and symptoms of illness and disease, as well as signs of mental illness and dysfunction. They understand growth and development and the application of this to a child's and teen's health. They are advocates for children's and teens' well-being in every sense of the word. They are in a unique position to partner with your child concerning his or her health. This is the time in children's development that forming a separate bond with their doctor can be of benefit to them. With your support, your child can be gently pushed to move in that direction.

"Isn't he [or she] too young?"

Whether a child or teen is too young for an independent chat with the doctor depends on what happens in the visit. If the doctor is examining a 12-year-old girl who has not yet begun menstruating, he or she will not be discussing whether the girl is sexually active and how she is ensuring her sexual health safety. But this age is not too young to begin to practice behaving as a young adult, to begin to learn how to express feelings and how to think independently about health decisions such as choosing healthy foods. This is a great time for pediatricians to engage with their patients and become trusted health care advocates for them. As your children mature, the scope of topics discussed in a well visit change to appropriately conform to their developmental stage.

"Will you be sharing this private and important information with me?"

The short answer is no. Although the actual law governing a minor's rights to confidentiality can be vague and vary from state to state, pediatricians respect a child's right to privacy and will protect it, except in the circumstance in which an adolescent discloses that he or she is being hurt or is looking to hurt himself, herself, or others. Legislation has expanded the rights of minors to make health care decisions for themselves. These laws were enacted to assist in situations in which notifying a parent would pose an obstacle to an adolescent's receiving necessary medical care. Sadly, not all families have healthy, open, and well-functioning channels of communication, and for those families, there needs to be a method of ensuring that, when necessary, a child's right to privacy will take precedence over a parent's right to know. Some examples of these circumstances include the following:

- Abortion
- Obtaining birth control
- Screening for HIV
- Treatment for AIDS and other sexually transmitted infections (STIs)
- Mental health problems
- Substance use and abuse
- Rape
- Incest or sexual abuse

However, a minor does not have unrestricted access to health care. The *mature minor doctrine* gives physicians some general guidelines for when they may provide medical treatment based on an adolescent's consent. (States vary on whether this is adopted as doctrine, but courts recognize the principle.)

The bottom line is that if an adolescent is in trouble, pediatricians will do the following:

- Assess the medical and emotional needs of the adolescent.

- Make recommendations on how to include the parent, including an offer to be the health communication liaison between a parent and an adolescent.

- Respect the wishes of the adolescent if the pediatrician feels there is cause to believe that the adolescent's rights to health care supersede the parent's right to know and the adolescent has sufficient maturity to support that decision.

You have worked tirelessly as a parent to raise a child who respects your values. Pediatricians know that because, in many instances as parents ourselves, we have done the same. In the end, though, children make independent decisions about which of their family's values they will choose for themselves. Your adolescent's physician will encourage him or her to share important physical and emotional health issues with you; however, there will be times that an adolescent will want something to remain private. Pediatricians are partners in your child's health care, and you can count on them to assist with his or her health care concerns.

"Why exactly do you need to do this?"

The question of why doctors need to meet with adolescent patients alone likely stems from fear on the parent's part. The teen years are the gateway to adulthood, and with that comes teens' desires to test their new wings. Adolescents are naturally more open about certain topics when parents are not listening simply because they might not want to disappoint or alarm their parents even if all they have are questions. Sometimes, an adolescent might have a very stressful and serious situation in his or her life that needs to be addressed and requires privacy and confidentiality. This guaranteed alone time with the pediatrician will allow and reassure the adolescent that there will always be an opportunity to discuss very pressing matters. Pediatricians typically use a tool called the HEADSS assessment (or other very similar tools) to address the different sensitive areas.

What Is the HEADSS Assessment?

An important aspect of any adolescent well-child visit is to explore the social well-being of that adolescent. To do this thoroughly, the HEADSS (*H*ome and environment, *E*ducation and employment, *A*ctivities, *D*rugs, *S*exuality, and *S*uicide) assessment, developed in 1991 by Eric Cohen, MD, and colleagues, is useful as a guide. Questions are tailored so they are suitable for the age of the child or teen.

Home and Environment

The pediatrician will ask the adolescent who lives in the home how things are going there. Many adolescents have difficulties, sometimes serious, at home. Pediatricians serve as safe havens for these kids because they talk about everyday problems that matter to kids. Sometimes pediatricians are more involved in more urgent ways when an adolescent confides about serious home life situations, such as physical or sexual abuse, neglect, and mistreatment.

Of course, it is impossible to know whether our patients are always being honest. Pediatricians pay close attention to body language, eye contact, and hesitation (or the lack thereof) when the patient answers questions.

Education and Employment

Pediatricians ask the adolescent in private about his or her school experience. Sometimes the difference between what was said with and without the parent present is telling and important. Some of the topics that come up include the following:

- School absences

- Academic performance problems that may involve undiagnosed neurobehavioral conditions such as attention-deficit/hyperactivity disorder and learning disabilities

- Desire to attend college, including specific concerns, fears, or questions about attending college

Activities

What an adolescent does to stay active is an important part of his or her health and one that many adolescents neglect. This is a great opportunity to review what they enjoy and how they can continue to stay active with a very stressful school schedule or extracurricular activities.

Drugs

Asking about drug use in front of parents is unlikely to yield an open, honest, and forthcoming response. If a parent believes that drug use is actually a problem for an adolescent, this well-child visit is an opportunity for him or her to get needed help. The pediatrician can advise your adolescent about how and where to get help and encourage him or her to include you in the process. Some concerned parents might ask the pediatrician to do involuntary drug testing on their adolescent. The American Academy of Pediatrics (AAP), along with many other national organizations, advises against this.

Substance Use Statistics in America

Adolescent substance use is a major problem in America. Alcohol, tobacco, and marijuana are the most used substances in the United States by children and adolescents. By the 8th grade, 28% of students have tried alcohol and 12% have been drunk at least once in their lives. The 2015 Youth Risk Behavior Survey found that among high school students during the prior 30 days, 33% drank some amount of alcohol, 8% drove after drinking, and 20% rode with a driver who had been drinking alcohol. Thirty-eight percent of high school students reported having used marijuana. Research shows that marijuana use can have permanent effects on the developing brain when use begins in adolescence, especially with regular or heavy use. Frequent or long-term marijuana use is linked to school dropout rates and lower educational achievement.

The AAP policy statement, "Substance Use Screening, Brief Intervention, and Referral to Treatment," recommends that pediatricians screen for substance use in adolescents at all visits and provide brief interventional care when appropriate. In addition, pediatricians should know how to make referrals for the treatment of more significant drug problems.

Getting to the Bottom

This one-on-one moment is when I ask specific questions about drug and/or alcohol use. The moment there is hesitation, I say to the teen, "I'll take that as a yes." The patient will usually chuckle and give me the details that I need so we can properly address this together.

One of the ways that pediatricians feel comfortable performing this screening properly is through the use of motivational interviewing (MI). The MI skills stress the use of open-ended questions, affirmation, reflection, and summarizing (OARS) as an evidence-based method of effective communication. Parents can use some of these same skills to speak effectively with their children and teens. See the "Motivational Interviewing" text box for types of questions you can try with your child.

Motivational Interviewing

OPEN-ENDED QUESTION:
These are questions that require more than "yes" or "no" responses.

"Can you tell me about the things that you enjoy doing with your friends?"

AFFIRMATION:
Highlight an individual's specific strengths and values that may lead him or her to make positive changes. Avoid phrasing affirmations as positive judgments, like "You're doing great!" which suggest that determination of what is good and bad is coming from a place of authority. The pediatrician is not positioning himself or herself from a place of authority but, rather, as a facilitator.

"I can see that if your friends like to get together and smoke marijuana, it must be very hard for you to say no."

REFLECTION:
Statements that summarize the individual's narrative without adding any judgment.

"I understand that you want to continue to be with your friends even though they may sometimes behave in ways that you are not entirely comfortable with."

SUMMARIES:
Combines different points made by the adolescent. The summaries check your understanding of what the person has said and are useful transitions between various points of the conversation.

"Let me see if I have this right; you are not happy with certain behaviors in the group that you hang out with, but you really like everything else about them. You don't feel that you will be influenced to use marijuana, and you also don't think that it affects your day-to-day life if they smoke around you."

After the HEADSS screening, pediatricians are able to determine whether the teen has a substance use disorder and the degree of that disorder. The range of substance use and the goals of the pediatrician in response to each stage are defined in Table 6-1.

Table 6-1. Substance Use Spectrum and Goals for Brief Intervention (BI)

Stage	Description	Goals
Abstinence	The time when an individual has never used drugs or had more than a few sips of alcohol.	Prevent or delay the use of substances through positive reinforcement and education.
Substance use without a disorder	Limited use, generally in social situations, with no related problems. Typically, use occurs at predictable times, such as on weekends.	Advise to stop. Provide counseling regarding the medical harm of substance use. Promote teen's strengths.
Mild–moderate substance use disorder	Use in high-risk situations, such as when driving or with strangers. Use associated with a problem, such as a fight, arrest, or school suspension. Use for emotional regulation, such as to relieve stress or depression.	Brief assessment to explore teen-perceived problems, associated with use. Give clear, brief advice to quit. Provide counseling regarding the medical harm of substance use. Negotiate a behavior change to quit or cut down. Provide close monitoring. Consider referral to a treatment center. Consider breaking confidentiality.
Severe substance use disorder	Loss of control or compulsive drug use associated with neurologic changes in the reward system of the brain.	As above. Involve parents in treatment planning whenever possible. Refer to the appropriate level of care. Follow up to ensure compliance with treatment and to offer continued support.

What Parents Can Do

Drugs are clearly a major topic for those who care for children. In 2011, a nationally representative household survey was conducted that revealed that drug abuse was the number one household concern of adults for the adolescent population.

As your child goes through puberty, start to create an open and welcoming environment that encourages discussion and offers nonjudgmental advice about drug use. In the early period of puberty, your child is a captive audience and will be receptive.

- Learn the facts about what kids are doing. Learn about alcohol use, marijuana, cigarettes, e-cigarettes, performance-enhancing substances, and many other products that adolescents think are somehow good for them.

- Ask them about their friends, get to know their friends, and try to be involved as much as you can.

- Have a relationship with your adolescent's friends' parents if possible. The more that your adolescent knows that you are aware of his or her activities and that you can call a friend's parents at any time, the better.

- Have age-appropriate discussions and limit the time; you will lose your adolescent's attention if the talk becomes a 2-hour event. Keep it short and plan to talk often. As your adolescent matures, make it clear that you will be there to listen if there is anything that he or she wants to discuss.

- Make sure that your adolescent knows that you will always be supportive, and make sure that you are supportive. If you break trust with your adolescent, you may never get it back.

- Be the person that he or she can come to about anything, with no fear.

- Always remember to be the person that you expect your adolescent to be. Do not think that you can sit around and smoke in front of your kids but advise them not to. You must be the person that you want him or her to emulate.

Sexuality

You may feel that you have some pretty contemporary ideas when it comes to sex and sexuality, but when it comes to your teenager, these things can be very uncomfortable and difficult. It's entirely understandable and natural. Having open and frank discussions about sex is extremely relevant to your teen's well-being. The AAP encourages parents to have open and honest discussions about sexual development, sexual desire, and the nature of an adolescent's developing sexual identity.

Taking opportunities to share factual information and give good moral guidance is a vitally important part of helping a teen understand himself or herself. It cannot be overstated what a great value this type of open relationship has and its potential to possibly help your adolescent avoid life-changing errors in judgment.

Although few would disagree that abstinence is the best method to stay safe and healthy until an adolescent is mature enough to "handle" an intimate relationship, reality tells us that this may be quite unrealistic. Accepting that our teens are offered an overwhelming array of enticement to jump into the sexual arena through advertising, media, and social media, we must do our best to balance these forces and provide a voice of reason. However, this can only be truly effective if we are able to provide nonjudgmental information and answers to questions that might privately make our hair stand on end. Parents and pediatricians need to stay educated and informed about the habits of today's youth. Learning how to offer guidance without lecturing should be key to your communication.

The following are some examples of the questions that pediatricians ask teens aged 13 years and older:

"Are you sexually active?"

According to the Centers for Disease Control and Prevention (CDC) 2015 Statistics on Sexual Risk Behaviors, 41% of all high school students have had sexual intercourse, and 30% had had sexual intercourse during the previous 3 months.

Although most teens are not partaking in sexual activity, there is a great deal of information that can and should be discussed for those who do or will partake. If teens are going to engage in adult activities, they should be educated on an adult level in advance of making such choices and be pushed to consider the adult consequences of such decisions.

"If you are sexually active, what protection are you using?"

According to the same CDC 2015 survey, 43% of all US high school students did not use a condom the last time they had sex, 14% did not use any method to prevent pregnancy, and 21% had drunk alcohol or used drugs before last having sexual intercourse.

"Do you know how to protect yourself against unwanted pregnancy?"

Worldwide teen pregnancies are down, but the United States continues to see substantially higher teen birth rates as compared with other developed countries. According to the same CDC 2015 survey, in 2014 nearly 250,000 babies were born to teen girls aged 15 to 19 years.

"Have you been tested for sexually transmitted infections (STIs)?"

Young people (aged 13–24 years) accounted for an estimated 22% of all new HIV diagnoses in the United States in 2014. Half of the nearly 20 million new STIs reported each year occurred in young people between the ages of 15 and 24 years.

The statistics on risky sexual behavior are overwhelming and continue to document how much adolescents need an open, honest, and loving relationship with their parents so that topics such as sexual orientation, sexual behavior, and their risks can be discussed. The AAP recommends that all sexually active adolescents be screened for STIs such as chlamydia. Chlamydia is the most prevalent illness, usually with minimal symptoms, and can result in pelvic inflammatory disease, which can result in difficulty conceiving or infertility.

Among young people aged 13 to 24 years diagnosed with HIV in 2014, 80% were gay and bisexual males. Any person who engages in unprotected sex and is not in a monogamous relationship with someone who recently tested negative is at high risk for contracting HIV. These individuals can benefit from understanding the value of pre-exposure prophylaxis (PrEP), which consists of taking medications on a daily basis and has been shown to significantly reduce the chance of HIV infection.

Motivational Interviewing Technique

A 14-year-old girl with limited financial resources came in for a well-child visit. During the course of the examination, I asked her if she was sexually active, and she answered that she was. I asked her about protection, and she informed me that a condom was used only some of the time. I asked her why she used protection only some of the time, and she stated that she and her boyfriend, who was 15, did not always have a condom available. When I asked her if it was her intention to get pregnant, she emphatically stated, "Absolutely not!" I explained to her that she would definitely become pregnant if she continued having unprotected sex and asked if she was prepared to be a parent. She again emphatically stated that she was not. I once more explained that the consequences of her very "adult" actions would undoubtedly yield some major adult responsibilities, such as raising a child or possibly getting a sexually transmitted infection. At this point she stated that she realized she should always use birth control, specifically a condom, but admitted that access and cost of condoms had been a factor in their lack of use.

The goal of using motivational interviewing (MI) techniques is to allow an individual to independently conclude what is best for himself or herself. I used an MI technique in my discussion with her and asked for her permission to speak more about the choices available to her concerning her sexual behavior, as well as her right to choose abstinence. I always work very hard to refrain from lecturing and to offer advice that would be welcomed by my patient. At the end of our discussion, I supplied her with a bag of condoms and advised her to come to me if she did not have access to more. She agreed to be screened for sexually transmitted infections and also to think about her choices concerning her sexuality.

As a mother and as a pediatrician, I know what you are thinking: "Are you kidding me? You can't be serious about speaking to a 14-year-old about her sexual relationship. You can't possibly keep that information from her parents. Don't you think that it is imperative to get her family involved? How could you give her condoms? Isn't that in direct conflict with her health and well-being?"

Of course, she is way too young to be sexually active and I am fearful about pregnancy, her health, and her well-being. However, first and foremost, to effectively help and guide her, I need to partner with her. This is the first important step in what I hope will be an ongoing close professional relationship built on trust and respect.

When an Adolescent Is Too Young

Most adolescents, like the girl in the example, are too young and emotionally immature to have a responsible sexual relationship, but this won't stop them. If a doctor tries to convince adolescents to simply abstain from sex, they might never trust the doctor about this or any other sensitive subject. The only chance the pediatrician has of getting a patient in this type of situation to do the safe thing is to be an advocate and someone with whom he or she can have a meaningful, honest, and nonjudgmental conversation. By listening to his or her needs and desires and asking if it would be all right to share facts about unsafe sex, the pediatrician does what is possible to have the adolescent recognize the value in waiting until he or she is emotionally ready. In this situation, teens have an opportunity to express how they feel and to ask questions. The doctor is available for additional discussions and to encourage frank discussions with parents. If the adolescent says "No," then the doctor continues to work with the teen alone.

The Reason Behind Not Informing Parents

By law, pediatricians and other doctors are not permitted to tell the parents of an adolescent anything unless the patient is at risk for hurting himself or herself or harming someone else. Even if informing parents of an adolescent's sexual activity without his or her consent were a legal option, the breach of confidentiality may seem like a betrayal and the adolescent might no longer confide in the doctor and might never trust an adult again. The more interesting thought is why parents are not able to discuss the difficult questions about sexual activity with their teens.

Why Parents Might Not Ask the Tough Questions

Parents might not ask questions about sexual activity or drug use because of fear of the answer. Or, it is possible that they do ask, and their teens might not answer honestly for fear of being punished or upsetting their parents.

Parents' fear of upsetting their teen is an important justification for using nonjudgmental behavior and motivational interviewing techniques when possible. It allows parents to have teachable moments rather than to lecture. Conflict simply results in missed opportunities and almost never encourages teens to change their behavior.

How a Pediatrician Can Provide Birth Control without Parental Permission

Providing birth control does not enable teen sexual activity. Doctors wish to protect their patients, including adolescents, as best they can. Adolescents who are already having unprotected sex will continue to have unprotected sex and risk pregnancy or sexually transmitted infections if not provided with protection. Doctors use MI techniques to help patients understand and consider other, much safer ways of having a meaningful relationship at this young age; however, to be successful, that discovery must come from the patient, not me.

What Parents Should Do

Be the kind of parent that your teen can come to with anything. Be available to listen and alert to situations when your teenager starts to open up about important topics. Teens have a way of bringing up important topics at rather odd times, so be ready. You may need to drop whatever you are doing, but it will be worth it. Listen more than speak and hold back your reaction. If you do inadvertently react, explain to your teen that this subject matter has caught you off guard and you need to absorb what is being said. Tell your teen that you might be a bit surprised by the problem but that you are not upset with him or her, and then reassure your teen that you want to help. Having a relationship with your teen that allows him or her to confide in you, get your advice, and feel your love is very important. It is best if you are the first line of defense.

What to Do if Your Daughter Has Unprotected Sex

It is possible to assist a teen in a compromised position after having a sexual encounter without protection. In 2012, the AAP came out with a new policy statement, "Emergency Contraception," that discusses how emergency contraception can reduce the risk of unwanted pregnancy in adolescents. The reasons for advocating or prescribing this medication include the following:

- Despite our best efforts to educate teens and prevent it, many teens continue to have unprotected sex.

- As many as 10% of teens are victims of unwanted sex, such as sexual assault.

- Although contraception has been used, it might have failed.

- Using emergency contraception medications such as Plan B or Next Choice within 120 hours of poorly protected or unprotected sex might be the only nonprescription method to prevent an unwanted pregnancy. This method works better when used within 72 hours after unprotected sex and works best within 24 hours.

- When necessary, prescription methods of emergency contraception, such as different types of IUDs or combination birth control pills, are available. Additionally, there is a prescription pill that, unlike the non-prescription medications, is just as reliable on the fifth day after unprotected sex as on the first day. Discuss this with your pediatrician if it should ever be necessary.

Emergency contraception medications are not able to protect against STIs, and they are certainly not a viable method of birth control, but your teen's pediatrician can help prevent an unwanted pregnancy in an emergency and offer appropriate counseling and STI testing.

Many teens will not speak about sexual encounters such as rape, harassment, or unwanted touching that may have occurred. It is important for both the parents and pediatrician to ask questions in a caring environment and give teens the opportunity to ask for help.

Gender Issues and Sexual Orientation

A person's sexual orientation is seen as a continuum with homosexuality at one end and heterosexuality at the other. An adolescent may be anywhere along this continuum; sometimes, sexual orientation does not settle in fully until adolescence is nearly complete. No wonder it is a confusing time!

Gender identification is separate from sexual orientation. Gender is a person's internal idea of who he or she is. Some individuals with the physical characteristics of a male feel on the inside that they are female, and vice versa.

Being Transgender

Not too long ago, I met with a lovely 13-year-old girl for her well-child visit. After her mother had left the room and it was just the 2 of us, she told me that she would really like to speak with a behavior health specialist. She said that she felt like she needed to talk with a professional about feeling sad. I assured her that I would help her with that and asked if we could complete a depression screening. The results showed only mild depression, and I found it a bit odd that she was so insistent on a referral when her level of depression was rather low. We continued to go through the different HEADSS categories of questions. I asked her if she was sexually active and she said she was not. I next questioned her about her sexual orientation and asked her if she had thought about whether she was attracted to women or men. She quickly answered that she was a lesbian and attracted to women. I then asked whether she had thought about her own gender and whether she considered herself to be a girl or a boy, or not sure. She answered that she considered herself to be a boy.

At this point, I asked her if her mother was aware of this and she said that she had shared many aspects of being transgender with her mom but had not told her directly how she felt. She wanted me to talk about the specifics with her mother and said that not being able to talk with her mother was why she was upset. She also told me that she had a group of wonderful and supportive friends. When I called her mother into the room and told her how her daughter felt, her mother was not surprised. She had suspected how her daughter felt but had chosen not to pressure her into talking because she wanted her daughter to tell her directly when she was ready.

Life as a lesbian, gay, bisexual, transgender, or questioning (LGBTQ) youth is difficult. Most teenagers find discussing sexuality with their parents to be very difficult. They may not even understand how they feel or how to talk about it. Many families are not accepting of gender or sexuality differences and this can create a difficult home life for LGBTQ youth.

Youth who are LGBTQ need an exceptional amount of support in navigating adolescence. They often face much ridicule and rejection specifically because of their sexual orientation. According to some studies, they are more likely to be threatened or injured with a weapon, skip school because of not feeling safe, and be bullied at school as compared to their heterosexual peers. More than half of all transgender students experience some sort of bullying or harassment at school. This kind of behavior can lead transgender students to feel isolated and can have long-lasting effects beginning now and into adulthood, including depression, self-harm, or even thoughts of suicide.

Suicide

Suicide has risen from the third- to the second-leading cause of death among adolescents. Now, only unintentional injuries, such as motor vehicle crashes and accidental poisoning, claim more teen lives.

The risk factors identified for suicide attempts include the following:

- A family history of suicide
- A history of physical or sexual abuse
- Mood disorders/depression
- Drug and alcohol use
- Lesbian, gay, transgender, bisexual, and questioning of sexual orientation identification
- Bullying
- Excessive use of the Internet, which is referred to medically as *pathologic Internet use.*

Our Future

. . . .

One day, adolescents will be the ones who protect our world, but that day is not here yet. There are many areas in which they are particularly ill-prepared for adulthood. Professionals trained to work with children, such as pediatricians, educators, psychologists, and other specialists, partner with you to find the best strategies to influence your children, our future.

The AAP and its approximately 67,000 member-pediatricians in the United States, Canada, Mexico, and many other countries, dedicate their efforts and resources to the health, safety, and well-being of infants, children, adolescents, and young adults.

There is no shame in alone time with the pediatrician. Parents who adamantly believe that they are not happy with their adolescent's "alone time" with the pediatrician, should realize how important it is to have intimate and clear dialogue surrounding delicate matters covered during the one-on-one period. I encourage them to try to have as open and honest a relationship with their teen as possible. It is wonderful if they can have frank discussions about all of the pressing matters that children and teens endure during puberty and beyond.

However, it is far from a defeat if that is not the case. Often, it requires someone who is removed from the emotional boundaries of parenthood to broach these topics. Sometimes, no matter how open a relationship a parent may have with a child or teen, there are some things the child or teen may only want to share with a professional, and that is OK.

PART

3

A Time to Value Health and Wellness

CHAPTER 7

Taking Control of Weight Issues

Struggling with weight issues is tough at any age, but struggling with weight issues and being an adolescent is particularly difficult. As a parent, it can be heartbreaking to watch your adolescent struggle. There are few stages in life when one is more vulnerable to feelings of desperation and dissatisfaction about his or her looks or how to improve them.

As you raise a child with a weight issue, you should try to be accepting of your child or teen and encourage him or her to accept himself or herself just as he or she is. However, you have an important responsibility to motivate your adolescent to consider implementing lifestyle changes that can reduce or eliminate the chances of encountering the many health risks associated with having an unhealthy weight.

Good health requires regular attention and depends on factors such as appropriate hydration, nutrition, physical activity, and sleep. The significance of caring about general health and wellness is described in more detail in Chapter 10, but it is essential to discuss here the value of maintaining a healthy weight. Many health risks are directly connected to an unhealthy weight, and you can have a positive effect on adolescents who must deal with weight issues.

Many different problems can result in an unhealthy weight, such as disordered eating or an eating disorder, as addressed in Chapter 2. In this chapter, we focus primarily on the issues surrounding having overweight or having obesity. In an effort to be sensitive to and respect the effort to reduce the stigma associated with using the terms *overweight* and *obesity*, I will use those terms only in conjunction with the medical diagnosis and refer to individuals with these conditions as having "unhealthy weight" when they are diagnosed as overweight and having "very unhealthy weight" when they are diagnosed with obesity.

No magic pill exists that can address unhealthy weight, but the perspective offered in this chapter may add more dimension to how you think about the obesity epidemic and ultimately how you can deal with weight issues that so often complicate puberty.

The Magnitude of the Problem

Data collected by the National Health and Nutrition Examination Survey demonstrate that between 2011 and 2014, 17% of youth had obesity. Approximately 21% of adolescents between age 12 and 19 years were found to have obesity. These statistics have nearly quadrupled since 1980. If we consider those individuals who have overweight, as well as those who have obesity, we find that nearly one-third of children and teens between the ages of 10 and 17 years are affected. These rates are even higher in Hispanic and African American communities. We know that teens who have overweight or obesity have a greater chance of becoming adults who have overweight or obesity than teens with no weight issues.

These statistics are shocking enough without delving into the consequences of unhealthy weight; however, the real tragedy lies in the fact that because of the health risks associated with obesity, the current generation of children and teens might well be the first to have a shorter life expectancy than their parents.

The bodies of individuals with type 2 diabetes make insulin but don't use it as well as they should. This is called *insulin resistance.* In the past, type 2 diabetes was a disease that affected middle-aged individuals with unhealthy weight. Until 2001, only 3% of all children newly diagnosed with diabetes were diagnosed with type 2 diabetes. Almost all were diagnosed with insulin-dependent diabetes mellitus (IDDM), or type 1 diabetes, which is the type of diabetes that requires an individual to take insulin daily for the rest of his or her life. It is not caused by unhealthy weight or an unhealthy lifestyle. It is a familiar disease of childhood. In the 1980s, IDDM accounted for nearly all new cases of childhood diabetes. Today, 45% of children diagnosed with new-onset diabetes are diagnosed with type 2 diabetes, up from 3% in 2001.

If type 2 diabetes develops in an adult between ages 55 and 65 years, and that person lives with it for 20 to 30 years without having particularly good glucose (sugar) control, which is influenced by proper diet, exercise, and lifestyle, many of the health consequences of diabetes will occur as that individual reaches 75 to 85 years of age.

These health complications include losing one's eyesight; loss of kidney function; immune system problems, including poor ability to fight and heal infections; heart disease; nerve damage; and more. These health problems can be devastating; however, they were somewhat invisible to the public because individuals with type 2 diabetes tended to develop the associated health consequences when they were no longer active, readily visible members of the community. In addition, people often thought these poor health effects were a part of getting old.

The fact that type 2 diabetes is affecting children and adolescents is reason enough to be concerned. But the challenges of living with type 2 diabetes as an adolescent are nothing compared to the long-term health risks that accompany the disease. As more adolescents are being diagnosed with type 2 diabetes, we can anticipate that after they have lived with the disease for 20 to 30 years, the side effects of poor glucose control will now take place during the prime years of their lives, as compared with past generations, who had these side effects as elderly patients.

Unhealthy weight, in addition to causing type 2 diabetes, also leads to other health problems. It is connected with high blood pressure, high cholesterol, liver disease, gallbladder disease, sleep apnea, asthma, cancer, depression, stress on the joints, and other illnesses.

Obesity is now the second leading cause of preventable death, only after smoking. In 2013, the American Medical Association took the important step of declaring obesity a disease. Considering obesity a disease has enabled the health care community to discuss, study, and consider treatment options that may help. It also means that insurance coverage is available for necessary treatment. Considering obesity a disease also helps to reduce some of the stigma associated with being at this very unhealthy weight.

The Stigma of Obesity

Teens experience a great deal of insecurities while going through the changes associated with puberty. Maintaining high self-esteem plays an important role in the well-being of any teen. When adolescents are dealing with having overweight or obesity, the stigma and discrimination they experience can create a huge barrier to positive development. It has negative implications for basic health, wellness, and quality of life. The unhealthy weight alone is a predictor of bullying, teasing, and victimization. In the school setting, weight-based bullying is among the most frequent forms of peer harassment reported by students. In fact, 71% of those seeking weight loss treatment say they have been bullied about their weight in the last year, and more than one-third indicated that the bullying has gone on for more than 5 years. Bullying is defined as unwanted behavior that can involve aggressive verbal or physical actions such as threatening, teasing, hitting, kicking, or spreading rumors. There is a perceived power imbalance; as such, children who are bullied may be weaker or small, possibly shy or helpless. Others can be at a higher risk of being bullied, especially those who are lesbian, gay, bisexual, or transgender. Bullying that occurs through electronic methods, via social media sites, texting, chat rooms, or instant messaging, is considered cyberbullying.

How to Address Bullying of the Overweight Child or Teen

- **No one deserves to be picked on!** Children and adolescents should understand that under no circumstances is it ever OK for anyone to be mean to or to physically threaten them.

- **Inform an adult.** Anyone who is ridiculed for any reason, including their weight, should notify an adult. For the younger kids, this adult is generally the parent. For teens, it might be a trusted adult at school, such as a counselor or teacher. In either age group, an adult needs to be involved.

- **Don't walk around alone.** The child or teen who is prone to bullying should keep his or her trusted friends close by, stay in a group, and try not to walk around alone.

- **Don't react to the bullying.** Unfortunately, when kids are upset, especially with obvious distress or outright crying, a bully may take advantage of the situation or be stimulated to continue. Staying in control is important. The child or teen should walk away whenever possible.

- **As the parent, involve a school official.** Teachers should know what is going on as soon as possible. Parents need to let the professionals know what is occurring and let them handle it rather than trying to address the situation with the bully's family. Many schools have defined anti-bullying policies. Bullying is unacceptable behavior, and adults in a position of authority should be made aware of and alert to the situation and be ready to help. If the child's or teen's parents have previously consulted with me about the bullying, I follow up with them about the school's response. If the reaction is still less than optimal, with the parents' permission, I write a letter as the child or teen's pediatrician in which I outline my position and the American Academy of Pediatrics (AAP) policies surrounding bullying.

- **Learn about all types of bullying.** Parents need to be sure that this behavior is not going underground with Internet-based attacks, also called cyberbullying. Cyberbullying is very difficult to deal with. Most schools also have cyberbullying policies.

How to Recognize and Stop Cyberbullying

Look for warning signs. Be aware of how your teen behaves while on the computer or phone. If you see agitated or angry behavior or school avoidance becomes an issue, consider talking to your teen. Try to listen and understand without jumping to conclusions. Help your teen feel comfortable by allowing him or her to explain what might be going on from his or her own perspective.

Keep your child involved. Keeping your child involved in the solution can help restore dignity, self-respect, and confidence and promote resilience in your teen. It is important to keep your teen in the loop, even if you need to have some private conversations with other personnel or school professionals. Make sure that your teen keeps all texts, e-mails, or screenshots of cyberbullying so they can be shared with those who can help him or her.

Think carefully. The way in which the problem is handled needs to be well thought out. Well-meaning parents can make the situation worse if they act impulsively without carefully thinking things through. Cyberbullying often involves somebody getting put down and excluded from other kids' activities. When a parent responds publicly or if the teen's peers find out about a meeting with school authorities, the marginalization can worsen.

Stay objective. Your first response is always going to be to protect your teen. However, you must try to be objective and find out all sides of the story before responding as objectively as you can. What you see online may only be one part of a much bigger picture.

Source: Adapted from http://www.connectsafely.org/

- **Consider activities outside of school.** The better and more confident a teen feels about himself or herself, the less likely he or she is to be a bully's target. Encourage older children and teens to look for outside interests to give them a new focus.

- **Listen to what your adolescent says.** Provide a strong support system for your adolescent and spend time together to reinforce how special he or she is and how proud you are of his or her strengths during this ordeal. Your adolescent needs to know that you will help him or her see this problem through. A bullied child's self-esteem needs your cheerleading; even older teens need to hear words of encouragement often.

- **Highlight your teen's strengths.** Parents need to spend time talking about their teen's qualities that they most admire. This is not superfluous. Your teen is very vulnerable at this time and filled with many ambivalent feelings of self-doubt. If your teen is willing, be open to discussing healthy ways to deal with his or her unhealthy weight while being sensitive and available. You can also consult your teen's pediatrician who is trained to help with situations like this and many others.

Zero Tolerance

There must be zero tolerance for abusive behavior. A person's physical and emotional well-being is at stake. In 2017, a jointly written policy statement, "Stigma Experienced by Children and Adolescents With Obesity," was released by the AAP and The Obesity Society to offer guidance for pediatricians and health care professionals to reduce weight stigmatization and discrimination and to educate others about the negative consequences of such actions.

Weight Conversations: Focusing on Health

Here are some simple ways to begin conversations about maintaining a healthy weight with your teen:

"Let's make this the year that we all get healthier."

"Everyone needs to pay attention to healthy habits, and it's time we thought about that as a family."

"What healthy habits do you think we could learn?"

"What would you like us to do as a family to be healthier?

"What do you think will be our biggest challenges to becoming healthier?"

"Let's talk about ways that we will resist those challenges."

"I'm excited about starting this together, what about you?"

Why Shaming Is Tolerated

Weight shaming is tolerated because most people, health care professionals included, often falsely believe that weight shaming helps motivate a person to lose weight. However, rather than motivating positive change, it is shown to have the opposite effect. Weight shaming contributes to behaviors such as binge eating, social isolation, avoidance of health care services, decreased physical activity, and increased weight gain, all resulting in worsening obesity and additional barriers to healthy behavior change. Furthermore, experiences of weight stigma dramatically impair the quality of life, especially for youth.

Recommendations by the American Academy of Pediatrics to Reduce Stigmatization

- Create healthy environments that effectively address and prevent obesity.

- Work together on healthy behaviors rather than reinforcing shame or stigma directed toward a child or teen with a very unheathy weight.

- Find out if your school has anti-bullying policies that include protections for students who are bullied about their weight. If such policies are not in place, parental efforts could help, as well as advocacy that parents can request of their health care professionals in reducing such bullying.

- Parents can involve themselves in efforts to advocate for a responsible and respectful portrayal of individuals who have obesity in youth-targeted media. By speaking out against stigmatizing depictions in the media, parents can help increase the awareness of weight stigma that can be particularly damaging to children and can reinforce the existence of broader societal stigma.

- Talk to your pediatrician about how to reduce weight stigma in all settings. Ask him or her to give you strategies to manage and address weight stigma in schools, communities, and at home. Parents can actively communicate with their children's teachers and school administrative staff to ensure that plans are in place to address weight-based victimization in their institutions. Parents can also determine whether potential weight stigma exists at home, where friends and family members can be sources of it.

- Finally, because the rates of obesity are higher in communities that are socioeconomically challenged and in communities of color, additional stigma attributed to race, socioeconomics, and sex could further compound the weight stigma experienced by some individuals, families, and communities.

Factors That Lead to Unhealthy Weight

Despite differences in culture, language, finances, and background, all parents share common questions, such as, "How did this weight problem occur?" and "How can I help my family lead a healthier lifestyle?"

When parents battle personal weight problems, there is a higher risk that they will have a child with an unhealthy weight as well. In fact, if one parent has obesity, the risk that his or her child also will have a very unhealthy weight is 3 times the risk in the average population. That risk jumps to 10 times if both parents have a very unhealthy weight. This emphasizes the importance of all family members maintaining a healthy lifestyle.

Children and adolescents with unhealthy weight are more likely to become adults with a very unhealthy weight problem. It is, therefore, important to appreciate the urgency in taking workable steps to improve the lifestyle of everyone in the household sooner rather than later. We know that the many health risks associated with very unhealthy weight in an adult are likely to be even more severe if the individual was a child with weight issues. Maybe the quickest and easiest workable step as a parent is to simply give yourself permission to have the patience to make small changes and stick with them. Next, decide on one small lifestyle change that you feel can work in your family. Regardless of what you choose, over time this becomes something to build on. You then become motivated to try a second change and then a third. Before you know it, you have made significant inroads in improving your family's lifestyle.

These suggestions are aimed at improving lifestyle behaviors and not focused on weight loss. As we discussed in Chapter 1, some children are at an unhealthy weight only as a result of the fat buildup that normally occurs prior to puberty commencing. As these children grow in height and maintain healthy habits, their weight in relation to their height will normalize.

Some of the best insights into parental perceptions of their children and their weight issues have come out of reports such as the one by Mott Children's Hospital in August 2007. In the Mott survey, children and teens who had a very unhealthy weight were identified. The children and teens

were divided into 2 age groups: 6 to 11 years and 12 to 17 years. The exam-
iners asked the parents to rate their child's or teen's weight by choosing
from the following categories: very unhealthy weight; slightly unhealthy
weight; about the right weight; or slightly under a healthy weight. The
parents were unaware that their child's or teen's weight had already been
determined to be in the very unhealthy weight category.

The results were quite astounding. In the 6- to 11-year age group, only 13%
of the parents saw their child correctly as having very unhealthy weight;
36% felt the weight was slightly unhealthy, 43% felt that their child was at
the right weight, and 8% felt that their child was under the healthy weight.

In the 12- to 17-year age group, 31% of the parents saw their teen correctly
at a very unhealthy weight; 55% felt their teen was at a slightly unhealthy
weight, 11% felt their teen's weight was about right, and 3% felt their teen
was under the healthy weight (Figure 7-1).

This survey overwhelmingly demonstrates the complications that parents
have in properly assessing their child's or teen's weight. Clearly for many
parents, there is a major disconnect between reality and their beliefs about
their children's weight. For these parents, this makes addressing weight
problems out of the question because they don't see a problem.

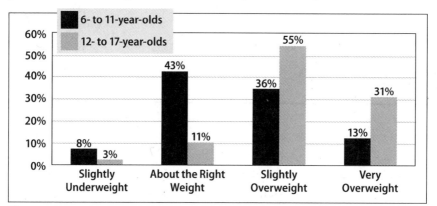

Figure 7-1. Parental Perception of Children's Weight Status for Children Aged 6 to 17 Years
Who Are Obese

Source: Davis MM, Singer DC, Clark SJ. Parental concerns about childhood obesity: Time for a reality
check? C.S. Mott Children's Hospital National Poll on Children's Health, University of Michigan. Vol 2, Issue
3, December 2007. Available at: http://mottpoll.org/reports-surveys/parental-concerns-about-child-
hood-obesity-time-reality-check.

Taking Action and Control
of Your Adolescent's Weight

As a parent, you are probably in the habit of assuming a good deal of guilt. Most parents are! Your teen may not have many healthy habits, but as you look at him or her, you may blame yourself for things that you imagine you did not do well or you could have done better. The blame game is very counterproductive. Later in this chapter we will look at some concrete modifications to lifestyle that are known to be helpful, and in Chapter 10, we will discuss additional recommendations that are considered best practice in helping children with the first steps to maintain a healthy lifestyle.

Parents can provide their children the first steps toward making healthy changes using the following guidelines:

- Eat 5 or more servings of fruits and vegetables daily.

- Create a Family Media Use Plan to help balance online and off-line activities (link provided in the Resources section at the end of this chapter).

- Schedule at least 1 hour of moderate to vigorous activity daily.

- Limit sugar-sweetened beverages.

Applying the Guidelines

Let's imagine that your teenaged daughter's meals are fairly regular and reasonably sized and include items such as chicken; healthy grains; occasional fruits; and, on a limited basis, vegetables. Her everyday lunch includes a bag of chips and, throughout the school day, a few cans of soda. Her weekly exercise consists of whatever is done in gym class on 2 of the 5 school days. As you look at the recommendations, you clearly see that she doesn't currently get the recommended 5 daily servings of fruits and vegetables and that she could be substituting some additional fruits or vegetables for her bag of chips. You also quickly realize that her daily exercise is not enough. As her parent, you can suggest she join a dance club after school or maybe find a Zumba workout that could be done at home a few times a week. These activities could take the place of some of her daily leisure screen time. Assuming there are sidewalks between home and school, the weather is reasonable, and it is safe to do so, why not suggest she add exercise time to her day by walking to school? Finally, offer her naturally fruit-flavored seltzer instead of soda, or better yet, encourage her to drink water more often.

These guidelines can help you and your family make meaningful changes quickly. Changes such as the ones described in this example would be a positive step toward improving your teen's lifestyle. The changes don't have to be made all at once. Have your teen choose one change and stick with it until he or she is comfortable, and then suggest that he or she pick something else that feels manageable. Making these types of focused small adjustments add up to a lifetime of better health. Studies show us that these rather small incremental changes hold the best value and have the greatest chance to endure. The most important thing to do is make the change a part of how you now live and stick with it instead of using it as a short-term fix. Making these changes for the entire family also ensures better success and reduces the stigma for the teen who is dealing with an unhealthy weight. These changes can benefit everyone, not just people with an unhealthy weight. Recommending healthy lifestyle habits is a prescription for everyone's health and well-being.

ChooseMyPlate Recommendation

Another recommendation for teens and families is ChooseMyPlate.gov, developed by the US Department of Agriculture (USDA) (Figure 7-2). The enormous amount of information found here is amazing, and it is all free! You will find countless pages of information that can help you understand food choices, portions, activity levels, and more. There are links to other valuable sites and more than enough resources to help you become an incredibly healthy individual.

At the ChooseMyPlate.gov Web site, you can find the most basic information about what foods make up a healthy diet and how much of each of these foods your teen should try to eat each day.

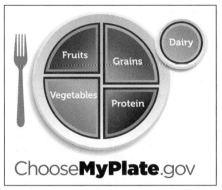

Figure 7-2. ChooseMyPlate.gov

Figure 7-2 shows how you can divide your plate into 4 sections. The 2 sections on the right are the grains and the protein. The 2 on the left are fruits and vegetables. You will also note that a small amount of dairy is considered. One of the first basic points about the foods that you choose is to fill half of the plate with fruits and vegetables. Because different fruits and vegetables offer different values, try to eat whole fruits and various types of vegetables to help you consume a variety of vitamins and minerals. At least half of the grains that you eat each day should be whole grains. Protein can be meat, fish, or plant based—it is a good idea to switch it up. With dairy, choose low-fat or fat-free products.

Another basic and important dietary tip is to limit the amounts of sugar, fat, and salt in the foods that you eat. Learning how to read and understand nutritional labels can be invaluable. The **ChooseMyPlate.gov** Web site offers terrific help with doing this.

Finally, there are tools to help you and your family start an athletic program and track your progress. It can be very motivating to have a way to track and celebrate the athletic accomplishments that you and your family are able to make.

Strategies for Weight Management

A lot can be gained by implementing healthy strategies that help individual teens and families improve their lifestyle. A discussion of healthy weight efforts is not complete without mentioning healthy strategies for weight loss and weight maintenance.

The single most important discussion to have concerns your teen's efforts to control weight, specifically, dieting. When it comes to your teen's weight and metabolism, there is hardly one solution. It may seem like many people around your child can consume large amounts of food and still maintain a consistent weight. This can be terribly frustrating if your teen does not have the same type of metabolism and his or her weight is hard to control. As people age, even those who have consumed mindfully might begin to see their metabolism slowing down. Eventually, you

Those Who Are Struggling

Being a teen is hard enough without weight problems. Although my focus is about how weight affects health, what most likely matters to your teen is simply how he or she looks. I wish that I could tell you that it is OK if your teen chooses to be a larger size. I'd love to say that it is your teen's decision and his or her life and that he or she should embrace whatever size feels good.

On a certain level, there are aspects to this attitude that are important and true; however, it just doesn't cut it when it comes to health, and I wouldn't be doing my job if I just left it at that. As a health care professional, a major part of my role is to educate parents and teens about health. I want you and your teen to be informed about the things that can and will have an important effect on health. I believe that everyone can make informed, smart decisions, but it is part of my responsibility to make sure that you receive the information that you need to make decisions about the best ways to keep the body healthy.

Right now, the emphasis is on inner beauty. Your teen may be comfortable in his or her own skin and I applaud that, but having an unhealthy weight is connected to many, many health problems and may be damaging your teen's potential for a future of well-being. This fact, and this fact alone, is the driving force for attempting to motivate everyone to consider changes to their lifestyle that have the potential to pay great health dividends later.

More information about the benefits of living a healthy lifestyle is in Chapter 10.

hear these adults mention that as kids they ate whatever they wanted and never gained a pound, while today they seem to gain weight more easily and need to be more conscious of their food choices. Healthy behaviors are not just for those who struggle. We all need to adopt healthy habits to maintain our health and fitness throughout life.

How Pediatricians Determine a Healthy Weight

How do doctors determine whether your teen's weight is medically healthy? They use a tool called body mass index (BMI) that measures body fat with a formula that considers your child's and teen's height and weight and then converts this information to a specific number. For children and teens younger than 20 years, that number is related to a corresponding percentile.

- If a teen's BMI percentile is less than the 5th percentile, he or she is considered underweight.

- A percentile from the 5th to less than the 85th indicates the teen is at a healthy weight.

- A percentile from the 85th to less than the 95th usually corresponds to having overweight or having an unhealthy weight.

The Health Risk Associated With an Unhealthy Body Mass Index

- Sleep disturbances
- Reflux or GERD (gastroesophageal reflux disease)
- Constipation
- Liver disease
- Gallbladder disease
- Menstrual abnormalities from polycystic ovarian syndrome
- Hip, knee, or leg pain from a weight-related disorder affecting the hip

- Foot pain from musculoskeletal problems in the feet
- Headaches from associated disorders in the brain
- Type 2 diabetes
- High cholesterol
- High blood pressure
- Depression
- Asthma

- If the teen's BMI is greater than the 85th percentile, the potential increases for problems related to general health and, depending on other factors such as family history and genetics, we know that the risk for health problems may be even that much higher.

- If the teen's percentile is greater than the 95th, he or she is considered medically obese or at a very unhealthy weight. The idea is not to pass judgment but to relate BMI to specific obesity-related health risks.

Avoiding Crash Diets

How can a teen begin to work on weight loss if his or her BMI suggests an unhealthy weight? First, emphasizing this as a *lifestyle change* is critical and should be viewed as getting healthy, fit, and strong, as opposed to thin or skinny.

When teens only work toward weight loss and neglect the importance of adapting a healthy, active lifestyle, they may concentrate on manipulating their eating by following different diets, many of which are neither healthy nor sustainable. In the short term, weight loss might occur, but it would not be worth the cost of what could happen to your teen's overall health! Moreover, although adhering to a diet can allow an individual to reach his or her goal weight, it typically results in instant rejoicing and the celebratory return to former eating habits.

Therein lies the problem. Those former eating habits may be part of what led to the unhealthy weight to begin with. When old habits return, so does the weight. Many kids with weight issues don't understand what it means to eat healthfully or maintain other healthy habits through adequate exercise, sleep, and hydration. All the effort to lose the weight, which could have amounted to starvation, counts for nothing and might even backfire when the teen's weight rebounds to an even more unhealthy level than before.

How To Begin the Hard Work With Your Teen

To take the first step, you and your family can ask yourselves four main questions.

QUESTION	RESPONSE
What and how much do you typically eat for your 3 basic meals?	
What and how much do you typically eat as your snacks?	
What and how much do you typically drink?	
What kind of exercise do you typically do and how often?	

The responses to these questions help to narrow down the areas in which the teen and family need to make the biggest changes. Some people pack away huge amounts of food at their 3 regular meals; some eat relatively healthy meals but go nuts throughout the day eating snacks and junk food. Others drink massive amounts of calories in the beverages they consume. Some just never get off the couch, and some have a combination of unhealthy habits.

Some teens are being completely truthful when they insist that they are unclear about their daily diet. They may suspect, but not know for sure, that they eat too much at meals or have an excessive number of snacks and drink unhealthy drinks. As a family you can sit down at night and each record in a notebook or on your phone what was eaten during the day, as well as each one's daily exercise. All of this material can be analyzed to determine how on-target your present habits are in leading a healthier lifestyle.

Your pediatrician can recommend a good nutritionist who can help you and your teen create positive eating habits. You also will find great material online at sites such as the USDA Web site (**https://www.usda.gov**) and **ChooseMyPlate.gov**, among others.

Although there is no single correct way to get things done, it is very important to stress that the process to successful change is easier when areas for improvement are identified. It is a good starting point and allows you to have a grasp on areas you and your teen need to focus on in your journey to develop a healthy, fit, strong, and sustainable lifestyle.

The Culture of Obesity

There is an overarching message in society that we all deserve to enjoy a healthy lifestyle, and yet, as we go through our everyday lives trying to make healthy choices for ourselves and our children, we encounter constant challenges that are in direct opposition to health and wellness ideals. These challenges come from a culture of obesity here in the United States.

The culture of obesity silently tempts poor health choices and undermines some of our best health-minded efforts. When we are aware of being manipulated and controlled by forces beyond our control, it can be empowering.

Recognizing the Culture of Obesity

The obesity epidemic is a complicated health issue that has many causes. Obesity is often looked at as an individual problem that needs to be solved by dealing with a person's behavior and possibly his or her relationships. Although there is no doubt that countless choices made by teens every day could be improved on, the influences (or, as I refer to them, "the forces") in society are just as important for concerned parents and their teens to consider. These forces are what cause wise health choices to be nearly impossible choices, especially for teens. Understanding the culture of obesity adds a new dimension to the struggle and hopefully empowers families and teens alike to find making the healthy choice easier. If we become aware of the presence of the culture of obesity, we will have an opportunity to reject it.

John Farquhar, MD, a cardiologist and the founder of the Stanford Prevention Research Center and Preventive Cardiology Clinic, was ahead of his time when he recognized that disease prevention might be affected by looking at its root cause from different perspectives. He made the following statement in 1987:

> "The growing urbanization and mechanization of modern life have made it easier for us to become physically lazy and sedentary. We drive rather than walk; we take an elevator rather than climb the stairs; we push a button on an electric dryer rather than bend down and reach up to hang clothes on a clothesline. Whereas exercise was once an inevitable part of living, today we must consciously plan to get the exercise needed to maintain good health."

Yes, we are more sedentary today than ever before. As Dr Farquhar reveals, there are many societal factors that have contributed to and resulted in this problem.

For our purposes, a *culture* is defined as the relationship between its core (the individual) and the 4 surrounding layers. These are the layers of causality (Figure 7-3). The layers that make up a culture and surround the core include the following:

- **Interpersonal Relationships:** relationships between the individual and others that affect the individual's behavior
- **Organizations:** made up of the schools we attend and places where we work
- **Community:** made up of the places where we live
- **Governmental Policies:** made up of the governmental influences (policies) that dictate how we live

Bronfenbrenner's Social-Ecological Model is often used to demonstrate the relationships between personal and environmental factors.

In Figure 7-3, I have used an adaptation of this model to illustrate the core layer surrounded and influenced by the layers of causality, each exerting forces that contribute to the culture of obesity.

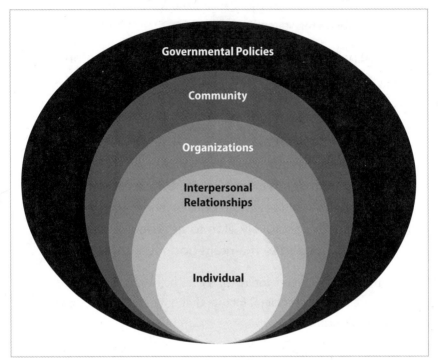

Figure 7-3. The Layers of Causality in the Culture of Obesity

Source: Adaptation of Bronfenbrenner's Ecological Systems Theory Diagram 1979. The McGraw Hill Companies, Inc (2010). Bronfenbrenner's Ecological Theory.

The Individual (the Core)

When we consider the role of the individual regarding weight, we take into account his or her daily lifestyle choices.

- What food choices, including beverages, does the individual make and how much is consumed in comparison with his or her energy needs?

- What level of activity does the individual have and how often does he or she exercise?

Although there are other considerations, these 2 questions give us a good insight into this person's lifestyle. Teens need to learn how to accept responsibility for making healthy lifestyle decisions, but if our culture was not a culture of obesity that places obstacles to health and wellness from the moment that we are born, making those good lifestyle decisions might not take the effort that it presently does.

The Interpersonal Relationships Layer

Jayvon is a 16-year-old student at a public high school. His mother, Ms Peterson, is a single mom who is working toward a secondary degree online. The family lives in a low-income neighborhood. Jayvon is a good student who works hard academically and tries to be supportive of his mom, whom he admires very much. At a recent well-child visit (also known as a *health supervision visit*), Jayvon and his mother were informed that Jayvon's weight, which has always been consistent with a healthy BMI, is now in the overweight category because he has crossed over the 85th percentile. Jayvon agrees that this information is important to him and says that he would like to make healthy lifestyle decisions, including paying attention to his food choices and trying to increase his exercise. He admits that it is difficult to always make healthy choices; however, he is going to try and wants to get better at it. At school today, his buddies ask if he would like to go out to eat at their favorite fast-food restaurant, and he happily accepts the invitation.

What is your reaction to this scenario? What strategies would you consider to help Jayvon make better "in the moment" choices going forward? How do you view this example in the context of society as a whole? Does society have any role in the lunch choice of this teen?

The interpersonal relationships that your teen has also play a big part in the lifestyle choices that he or she makes. A teen is affected by the family's attitudes and values, as well as the influence of friends and other contacts, such as in the following scenarios:

- Weekly, the teen's family loves to eat at establishments that feature huge portions of predominantly unhealthy foods.
- The teen's favorite activity with friends is to play video games for hours on end.
- In our example above, Jayvon's friends love to eat fast food. This exerts great influence on Jayvon and the choices he makes.

These relationships can have a huge effect on the family's health and wellness and the possible development of weight issues. It is possible for families to consider specific actions that will encourage a healthy, active household. The following are some examples:

- **Eat meals together as a family.** Research indicates that there is a relationship between regular family meals and the quality of food choices that adolescents make. The increased frequency of family meals is associated with greater intake of fruits, vegetables, and milk. Family meals will usually result in a decreased intake of fried foods and carbonated beverages. Eating together as a family is also associated with eating more nutrients such as calcium, iron, vitamins, and fiber and less consumption of saturated and trans fats.

- **Limit sweetened beverages.** Strong evidence shows that there is a link between the intake of sweetened beverages and obesity in children and teens. In January 2004, the AAP Committee on School Health released a policy statement that said that a clearly defined, school district-wide policy that restricts the sale of soft drinks will safeguard against health problems as a result of the excessive drinking of soft drinks and that pediatricians should work to eliminate soft drinks' availability in the school setting. Students should be encouraged to drink water and have limited intake of sugary beverages. Fruit juice should be 100% natural juice, but even this should be consumed in small amounts. Fruit's greatest value is realized when consumed whole and the nutrients, including the natural sugar, are mixed with the fiber in the fruit.

- **Encourage more fruits and veggies.** Everyone should eat 5 or more servings of fruits and vegetables each day. This is one of the major points you will see whenever obesity prevention for children and teens is discussed. Findings from Academy of Nutrition and Dietetics (formerly known as the American Dietetic Association) research show that eating more fruits and vegetables plays a significant role in preventing obesity in children and teens. Fruits and vegetables offer many nutritional benefits, and if young people eat more fruits and vegetables, they may eat fewer unhealthy foods. Fruits and vegetables are low in calories and high in fiber, have high nutrient density, and provide essential vitamins (eg, vitamins A, C, K) as well as potassium and magnesium.

- **Provide healthy choices that are readily accessible.** This seems like a simple fix, and it can be. Just having fresh fruits, vegetables, nuts, and seeds, as well as other good choices, readily available has been shown to affect whether kids eat these foods. Placing fresh fruit in bowls on the counter instead of keeping it in the fridge in can help tremendously in helping the family to remember to eat it! Cutting up vegetables into bite sized (non-choking size) portions or sticks and keeping them in a small container is also helpful.

- **Involve the family in food choices and cooking.** When kids have a stake in what is purchased and a role to play in food preparation, they are much more likely to eat the food. Among the many additional valuable skills this promotes are independent thinking about good food choice, awareness about the responsibility of meal preparation, awareness of financial concerns associated with choosing foods and ingredients, and math skills via the real-life activities connected to properly interpreting a recipe.

- **Encourage structured eating.** To maintain a healthy weight, it is recommended that children and teens eat 3 meals a day with 1 or 2 healthy snacks per day. Parents can help by ensuring that mealtimes such as dinner are kept at or around the same time each night so their child or teen knows and can avoid eating beforehand. Skipping meals may decrease a teen's level of energy, impact his or her level of concentration at school, and lead to additional snacking.

- **Eat slowly.** Feeling full requires more than our stomachs taking in a certain quantity of food. Our brains need to recognize we have eaten enough food. When we eat in a frenzy, we don't allow our brains to catch up with our stomachs. This may cause us to continue eating because our brains are not satisfied. Eat slowly and enjoy your meals. It takes about 10 minutes following a meal to recognize fullness, so wait at least 10 minutes before having dessert, and you may find that you eat it more sensibly.

- **Do not have a "clean plate" rule.** Whatever good intentions were associated with this rule, they have outlived their usefulness. As a society, we often overeat, have a distorted perception of normal portions, and emotionally value food in a destructive manner. Teaching your child or teen to clean his or her plate, as opposed to learning to appreciate feeling satisfied, is a major contributor to the development of weight issues. All children should be encouraged to eat what feels comfortable and then stop.

- **Avoid highly processed foods.** Highly processed foods include prepared meats, white bread, cookies, chips, soda, pasta, and candy. Examples of unprocessed or minimally processed foods include fresh or frozen vegetables, fresh meat, milk, eggs, and dried beans. Although many Americans consider highly processed foods to be very tasty, affordable, and convenient, the sugar, fat, salt, and flavoring in these foods may be a factor in overeating and a contributor to obesity. There should, however, be a clear distinction between these unhealthy, highly processed foods and processed foods such as canned vegetables and whole grain cereals, which have an important place among nutritionally sound, convenient food choices.

- **Encourage exercise.** Adolescents should engage in 60 or more minutes of physical activity daily. Most of this time should include moderate-intensity aerobic activity; however, at least 3 days per week, some vigorous physical activity should be included as well. For more information on key physical guidelines for children and adolescents, consult the USDA and US Department of Health and Human Services Web sites (see the Resources section at the end of this chapter).

- **Monitor screen time.** Increased sedentary behaviors, particularly watching TV, are a factor in the development of overweight children and teens. This finding is independent of the amount of physical activity that a child or teen gets. Spending many hours in front of the TV prevents physical activity and promotes mindless munching! Sitting in front of the TV promotes snacking outside of mealtimes and increases a child's or teen's exposure to countless food marketing ads for predominantly unhealthy foods. For more information on screen time, see the link to the AAP Media Plan in the Resources section at the end of this chapter.

- **Avoid emotional eating.** Avoid the trap of mindless eating! Emotional eating is common in our society. It is not healthy to eat highly processed sugary, fatty, salty, and calorically charged snacks while sitting in front of the TV and enjoying a sports event or a movie. Overcome this pitfall with healthy snacks such as celery, carrots, cucumbers, sliced peppers with salsa, unbuttered and lightly salted popcorn, or a bowl of berries.

- **Avoid an authoritarian parenting style** (see Parenting Styles text box).

Parenting Styles

The most important interpersonal relationship for any child is with the parent. Parenting style plays an important role in keeping your child or teen at a healthy weight. The following 4 parenting styles are recognized today:

Authoritative—This type of style includes setting clear limits and rules with balanced expectations, promotes independence, and includes warm responses within a supportive manner. A parent who has an authoritative style can be demanding of their child or teen, yet flexible and responsive to their child's or teen's needs and wishes.

Authoritarian—This type of style includes high expectations and strict rules that are to be followed without question. A parent with this style is demanding of the child or teen and may not be responsive to his or her needs or wishes.

Permissive—This style consists of warm responses and does not include setting limits, rules, or clear expectations. A parent who is permissive is not demanding of his or her child or teen, yet is responsive to the child's or teen's needs and wishes.

Disengaged—This style is not warm or responsive. A parent with this style does not set limits, rules, or expectations for his or her child or teen. A parent who is disengaged is neither demanding nor responsive to their child and is uninvolved or unattached entirely.

Adolescents need a supportive environment if they are to be successful in making big lifestyle changes. The authoritative parenting style has been shown to have the healthiest outcomes. Its associated outcomes include higher academic performance, increased self-esteem, minimal mental illness, enhanced social skills, and fewer delinquent behaviors. On the other hand, the authoritarian style has been linked to lower academic outcomes, poor self-esteem, increased mental illness and drug and alcohol use, and fewer social skills.

When parents understand the role that a parenting style can play in a child's or teen's health, they can use this information to evaluate their own style. They can then monitor and consider ways to more effectively reinforce their child's or teen's healthy eating habits and physical activity.

The Organization Layer

What role does this layer of causality play in influencing both individual and interpersonal choices? How does this affect our ability to keep up with healthful strategies and lifestyle success?

The organizational layer refers to our places of work or, in the case of our teens, where they attend school. How do organizations, particularly schools, play a role in contributing to the unhealthy weight issues that we have in America?

Given that our teens are spending the bulk of their productive waking hours at school, it is imperative that the healthy lifestyle considerations that are backed by research be supported—and certainly not undermined! Across the United States, many schools are not providing children with physical education (PE) on a daily basis, opting to limit it to only a few times a week or even eliminating it altogether due to budget cuts. Standardized testing mandates are a big barrier to PE in schools. Federal laws promoting academic skills have resulted in many schools cutting PE and recess out of the curriculum. Children who are allowed time for recess can potentially satisfy up to 40% of the daily requirement of physical activity. About a quarter of teens participate in at least 60 minutes of physical activity each day of the week. Despite challenges in PE programs and budget cuts, schools can play a proactive role in continuing to look for ways to provide as much physical activity as possible during the school week.

Schools and parents need to partner together in understanding the value of and promoting regular physical activity. In today's culture it is unlikely that your child or teen will receive the necessary amount of physical activity without this type of cooperation. Parents can explore what their specific district's policies are regarding the physical education curriculum. But make no mistake about this situation: the research overwhelmingly shows that active kids do better throughout their lives (Figure 7-4). It is strikingly clear that a healthy, active lifestyle has benefits that compound themselves throughout one's lifetime. Along with all the benefits noted in Figure 7-4, as active children and teens become

Physical Activity Behaviors of Young People

- In the United States, only 21.6% of children and adolescents aged 6 to 19 years attained 60 or more minutes of moderate-to-vigorous physical activity on at least 5 days per week.

- Today, nearly one-third of third graders do not get the recommended 20 minutes of daily recess, and students of color get even less.

- In 2015, 53.4% of high school students participated in muscle-strengthening exercises (eg, push-ups, sit-ups, weight lifting) on 3 or more days during the week.

- In 2015, 51.6% of high school students attended physical education classes in an average week, and only 29.8% of high school students attended physical education classes daily.

Sources: Kann L, McManus T, Harris WA, et al. Youth Risk Behavior Surveillance—United States, 2015. *MMWR Surveill Summ.* 2016;65(6):1–174; Aspen Institute Project Play. *Sport for All, Play for Life: A Playbook to Get Every Kid in the Game.* Washington, DC: Aspen Institute; 2015:9 & 18. https://assets.aspeninstitute.org/content/uploads/2015/01/Aspen-Institute-Project-Play-Report.pdf. Accessed February 23, 2018

active adults they will have lower morbidity and one-third lower disability levels. We also know that children of active moms are twice as likely to be active themselves. This leads to intergenerational change and can contribute to a process that affects our culture of obesity.

The time to promote an active and healthy lifestyle is from the moment that a child is born. Helping all children develop athletic or active lifestyles is a gift that pays dividends for a lifetime. When we talk about the effort needed to help children learn and love to be physically active for life, we refer to this as promoting *physical literacy.* Physical literacy refers to making sure that by the time all children are 12 years old, they have the ability, the confidence, and the desire to be active for life. Promoting physical literacy is a major step toward successfully affecting our culture of obesity. As a society, we need to raise a generation of kids who value and desire being active. It is already recognized that there exists today a huge decline in sports participation as kids reach puberty, and we need to provide active alternatives to sports, such as kayaking, biking, running, hiking, or skating, for those who are not interested in competitive sports.

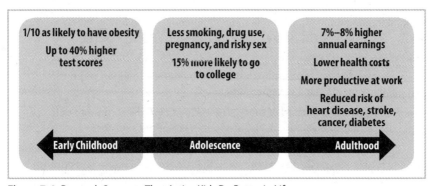

Figure 7-4. Research Supports That Active Kids Do Better in Life

Source: Adapted from the Aspen Institute Project Play: Sport for All Play for Life. https://assets. aspeninstitute.org/content/uploads/2015/01/Aspen-Institute-Project-Play-Report.pdf. Page 18.

Athletic educators, coaches, and health instructors play a large role in ensuring children are provided access to the physical literacy skills that will allow them to learn and value these skills. It also gives children an opportunity to understand and implement healthy lifestyle habits at an early age. By the time children are adolescents, the optimal time to build a love of athletics or physical literacy has passed. By the time puberty is reached, we have lost many opportunities to capitalize on all the benefits of regular physical activity, such as enhancing cognitive skills, health improvements, and physical well-being and enjoyment. Of course, it is never too late to make healthy lifestyle changes, but understanding the very broad benefits of physical literacy will hopefully inspire parents to advocate for changes to their school district's curricula.

Physical Literacy

The goal of physical literacy is to incorporate a structured curriculum for children from the youngest ages, within the school system and in athletic programs, that systematically teaches the athletic skills needed to allow any child, regardless of inherent talent, physical abilities, or lack of ability, to be physically literate by age 12 years and to have the tools to be active for life. Through its Project Play program, the Aspen Institute has developed the Sport for All, Play for Life model, which discusses and outlines how and why physical literacy is so critical and highlights the importance of recognizing that adolescents are leaving sports. The program also acknowledges the effect this has on adolescents' health and future health, as well as the potential health problem this poses to us all.

The Sport for All, Play for Life Model

The Sport for All, Play for Life model is a modified version by Project Play of the original model pioneered in Canada. Its goal is to reflect the needs of children in the United States and have every child be physically literate by age 12 years. This means that by age 12, every child will have the *ability, confidence,* and *desire* to be active for life.

- **Ability:** The competence in basic movement skills and overall fitness that allows a person to be able to engage in a variety of games and activities. Children will acquire this ability with a mix of informal play and the intentional teaching of specific movement skills, such as running, balancing, gliding, hopping, skipping, jumping, dodging, falling, swimming, kicking, throwing, and a range of skills that require hand–eye coordination.

- **Confidence:** Knowing that one has the ability to play sports or enjoy other physical activities. It is the result of programs or venues that include individuals with differing abilities and the support and encouragement from parents, guardians, coaches, administrators, teammates, and peers throughout the development process.

- **Desire:** The intrinsic enthusiasm for physical activity, whether in organized or unstructured formats, in traditional or alternative sport. This result is achieved through early positive experiences that are fun and motivate children to do their best.

The AAP recommends that schools support the development of lifetime sports. Lifetime sports are those activities that can be done throughout one's lifetime, such as running, swimming, and biking.

By the time teens reach high school, there has been a huge drop-off in the number who engage in organized sports. If lifetime sports were taught more in schools, the average child, not just the athletically gifted child, would be proficient and have the capacity to continue with athletics well into and beyond the teenage years.

National Efforts to Address Physical Literacy

Efforts are taking place nationally to improve the state of physical education and physical activity in our nation's schools. One such effort is the Whole School, Whole Community, Whole Child (WSCC) model, which can also help shape lifelong physical activity behaviors. Figure 7-5 demonstrates the 5 components of a Centers for Disease Control and Prevention (CDC) Comprehensive School Physical Activity Program (CSPAP).

The CDC recommends a multicomponent approach by which school districts and schools use all available opportunities for students to be physically active, meet the nationally recommended 60 minutes of physical activity each day, and develop the knowledge, skills, and confidence to be physically active for a lifetime. The goal of CSPAP is to increase physical activity opportunities before, during, and after school and increase students' overall physical activity and health. School health programs based on WSCC or coordinated school health models that include safe, supportive environments and engagement from communities and families as key components have been linked to improved academic achievement outcomes among students.

Providing Healthy Nutrition

Nearly half of all middle schools and high schools in the United States allow advertising of less than healthy foods, which directly affects a child's or teen's ability to make healthy choices. In response, many parent groups have called for a ban on advertising in schools. In 2004, Boston banned sugary drinks in public schools; researchers found that after the policy change took place, city students cut back on sugary drinks outside of the school environment as well.

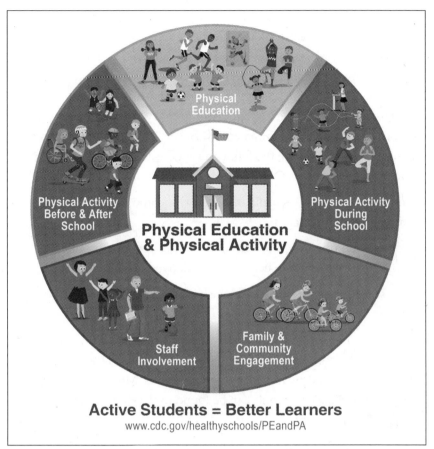

Figure 7-5. The 5 Components of a Comprehensive School Physical Activity Program

Our teens spend much of their time in school. Even if you are relatively successful at providing a healthy, active lifestyle at home, your teen may fail to follow these lifestyle choices at school simply because it is too difficult. Our teens should not have to struggle to maintain healthy habits when they enter their schools.

Schools and parents need to take responsibility for providing a healthy diet to our teens. Parents need to do their part in providing nutritious foods at home; however, for teens who eat at school, one option is to have access to more salad bars with fresh fruits and vegetables, which would go a long way toward increasing consumption of the daily requirements for fruits and vegetables. A recent study with younger children demonstrated that when salad bars placed in schools were decorated with familiar superheroes, the kids took significantly more salad items than when they were simply placed undecorated in the cafeteria. Similar advertising tactics aimed specifically at teens' interests, such as endorsement of healthy foods by favorite celebrities or sports figures, might work equally well. Teens would have a great opportunity to try different healthy foods with other teens in a welcoming environment. Parents should encourage schools to consider taking the following actions to improve the quality of foods offered on their premises if these do not already exist:

- Impose a ban on advertising unhealthy food and promoting unrealistic body images.

- Remove vending machines that carry unhealthy food products or replacing products with healthier alternatives.

- Ask school employees to model the health and wellness ideals that are taught to teens.

- Promote a culture of health and well-being in as many ways as possible. This could include ideas such as placing a ban on the distribution and sale of unhealthy foods on school grounds. More information on Smart Snacks in Schools can be found in the Resources section at the end of this chapter.

The Community Layer

The third layer of causality is community. Communities in which we live can be a force that either encourages or discourages our healthy lifestyle efforts. In a community, the healthy choice may not be the easiest choice. For instance, a low-income neighborhood may have difficulty providing access to regular outdoor physical activity. Parents can work with neighbors and other parents to find ways to push for improvements to community standards.

What can communities do to improve access to safe places to play in a neighborhood without them?

- Work together to have schools keep their grounds available after hours.

- Create policies to promote the building of safe streets and places to play.

- Work to get support and assistance to improve transportation and infrastructure (eg, sidewalks, crosswalks, traffic signals).

- Make a group effort to encourage the improvement of standards for healthy food choices in schools (promoting the availability of healthy food choices and eliminating unhealthy food marketing and food products and beverages such as those in vending machines).

In addition, communities should insist on healthier neighborhoods, in part by limiting the targeting of certain neighborhoods as desirable locations for fast-food establishments. Families need much greater access to healthier products that cost less; community leaders and local government can help with this. Finally, there should be a concerted effort to improve health literacy in neighborhoods so that the average person has a better understanding of what living a healthy lifestyle means. One way to approach this is via the media and joining organizations or clubs and school campaigns, as well as other local events, where information on healthy active living recommendations are produced and distributed through flyers, mailings, or community events that are culturally sensitive and tailored to meet the literacy level of the community as a whole.

What are some of the factors responsible for creating neighborhoods where unhealthy fast-food choices reign? This discussion begins first and foremost with understanding the role of unhealthy food marketing techniques.

Unhealthy Food Marketing Techniques

From the moment that we are born, we are exposed to the influences of food marketing. Food marketing to children is a nearly $2 billion a year effort; less than 3% of that marketing goes toward advertising healthy foods.

Food campaigns are often designed with deceptive techniques for young children to promote the development of food preferences for unhealthy foods that are rich in sugar, salt, and fat. Consumption of these foods makes young children feel happy, possibly resulting in an addiction to these foods. Also, the addition of sugar in various forms (high fructose corn syrup, evaporated cane juice, glucose) are ways of adding sugar to the diets of unsuspecting consumers. Peanut butter, ketchup, and salad dressing are examples of foods that surprisingly contain a great deal of added sugar.

Many health advocates feel very strongly that food marketing targeted to children younger than 8 years should be banned in much the same way as tobacco ads. Children in this age group are incapable of realizing that they are being manipulated. They are made a captive audience without being able to consent to it.

Once formed, food preferences follow us through life. When adolescents are faced with being able to make their own food choices at school, they struggle to make healthy choices. They know what foods they should be choosing, and they know why, but they simply cannot stop themselves in the moment from eating the foods they love or eating portions that are larger than the recommended healthy size.

Promoting Positive Change in Adolescent Behaviors: A Study

A study presented in the *Proceedings of the National Academy of Sciences* specifically addressed how to capitalize on typical and predictable adolescent behavior in an effort to promote positive change in their food choices. Results were quite astounding.

The researchers went to a middle school in Texas and randomly assigned 489 eighth graders to 2 different groups. Students in Group A were provided with a typical article on healthy, active living concepts. They were shown pictures of healthy foods and given details about the benefits of making good choices. Students in Group B were provided with an article that discussed the deceptive marketing techniques that are used to entice food sales for predominantly unhealthy foods. The article also discussed how certain additives in foods, such as sugar, salt, and fat, make the development of unhealthy food preferences likely and very difficult to change. The study positioned those in control of these marketing campaigns as authoritative, controlling adults and subsequently positioned the rejection of junk food as a method of rebellion against this control.

After classes concluded, all students attended a school-wide event that had no connection to this study. At the event, students were invited to choose from various snacks. The healthy options consisted of carrots, fruit, or trail mix, as well as water; the unhealthy options consisted of chocolate cookies, tortilla chips, or puffed cheese snacks, and soda or sugary fruit drinks. Those in Group B picked a significantly greater number of healthy snacks over the unhealthy snacks as compared with Group A.

Results of this study suggest that providing conventional straightforward education on the value of healthy foods *does not* have the same effect in motivating teens to make healthy choices as does providing information structured toward criteria that are key to the adolescent mindset. This includes rejecting authority, supporting defiance, and supporting community efforts. Framing the avoidance of junk food as a way to rebel against authoritative figures has an important effect. Teens can be influenced to make healthy choices when they are presented with information that resonates with them. By positioning the information as was done in this study, the researchers made the healthy choice the one that rejects authority, supports defiance, supports the community, and rebels against the control of authoritative adult figures.

It is unclear whether this type of approach will result in significant, long-lasting positive change, but it certainly suggests that it may resonate loudly with this age group. Capitalizing on the adolescent mind-set is a great way to effect positive change.

Read more about how to encourage healthy habits in your own home in Chapter 10.

What Parents and the Community Can Do

It is time for parents to come out in full force at school meetings and address the areas that are important to them. Among the topics to discuss are the following issues:

- Work with education leaders to ban unhealthy food advertising in schools. If your school has unhealthy food advertising in it, consider starting a concerned parent and student group. Talk about the points that are addressed in this book and refer to resources included at the end of this chapter. Another good resource with related tips for parents is the USDA Web site. Together you can ask to speak with school administration and voice your concerns.

- Work with city planning officials to limit the number of fast-food restaurants allowed in neighborhoods. Concerned parents can organize into groups, appealing to their local PTA or community centers to address the health needs of their community. Schedule a time to meet with city planning officials and be prepared to present your concerns in a professional manner.

- Increase access to healthy foods in neighborhoods by encouraging farmers' markets and other healthy options. Many neighborhoods lack access to healthy foods, but that doesn't mean that the healthy foods can't come into the neighborhood. For example, in the Bronx, a New York City borough, the Shop Healthy NYC initiative launched in 2012. This program involved 170 out of 200 corner grocery shops that agreed to participate to stock their shelves with healthy foods. Sales of healthy foods rose by 59% since this time. Parents can try to petition for similar programs to be considered in their neighborhoods.

- Push for affordable pricing for healthy foods. Here is a list of important ways to reach affordable pricing through different channels.

  - Establish a Food Policy Council

  - Encourage families to enroll in the Supplemental Nutrition Assistance Program (SNAP)

- Petition local officials to support the sale of local healthy foods across your community by offering incentives to small grocery stores and other neighborhood establishments that cooperate and stock shelves with nutritious choices, while also encouraging the establishment of farmers' markets.

- Request policies that support and protect community gardens.

- Request that food policies for food and beverages at schools purchased with government funds meet certain nutrition standards.

■ Work with school officials to add healthier menu options. Many schools have strong restrictions on their ability to control their menu choices, but you might be able to improve the quality of food served at school. Ask your school to look into the Salad Bars to Schools program and apply online. Or, maybe your school can consider using school grounds to make a working garden where teens can learn how to grow their own foods, helping them become interested in healthy eating and healthy living. Farm to school programs enrich the connection that communities have with fresh, healthy food and local food producers by changing food purchasing and education practices at schools. Students gain access to healthy, local foods as well as education opportunities such as school gardens, cooking lessons, and farm field trips. Farm to school programs empower children and their families to make informed food choices while strengthening the local economy and contributing to vibrant communities.

■ Develop a group to look into the value of a transparent "farm-to-fork" food supply. The Los Angeles Unified School District (LAUSD) is the largest public-school district in California, serves more than 650,000 meals a day, and spends $125 million on food each year. In the past, they served substandard meals without paying attention to meeting evidence-based nutritional standards. However, that has all changed now. The LAUSD created a farm-to-fork food program through the Good Food Purchasing Program. The program directs tens of millions of dollars in taxpayer funds spent on institutional food to support 5 overarching values: local economies, environmental sustainability, fair labor practices, animal welfare, and healthy food.

The policy was developed in 2012 by the Los Angeles Food Policy Council with input from multiple stakeholders. To develop such a program in your school district, contact local legislators and discuss the points contained in this chapter to aid in your efforts.

- Improve the state of physical activity within the community. An organized effort by parents in Seattle to create safe routes for younger teens to go to and from school and to help kids exercise regularly resulted in the implementation of "bike trains." Bike trains are led by adults, with one adult at the front and one at the rear of the train, and accompany students biking to and from school. A bike train can be set up with 1 or 2 adult neighbors biking together or even as a set route with multiple stations where more riders join in. Bike trains can be a great way to instill a love of bicycling in kids as they develop lifelong safety skills. Another way to improve the state of physical activity in your community is to organize specific committees dedicated to addressing different focus areas of change. As a group, ask your school to join the Presidential Youth Fitness Program. It will give your school an evidence-based, effectively coordinated, and strategically planned school health program.

- Join groups on social media and make your voice heard. Change begins when you make your voice heard.

The Governmental Policies Layer

Governmental policies can be supportive of healthy environments or can hinder them. Despite multiple positive messages from various government organizations like the USDA and Centers for Disease Control and Prevention, there is a clear failure to support health and well-being, especially in minority neighborhoods. Adolescent health and well-being can benefit from the following potential governmental policies that do not currently exist:

- Setting school food standards in all schools

- Restricting unhealthy food marketing to children

- Taxing certain unhealthy foods

- Supporting legislation that would make consumer friendly nutritional labeling even better than it is today

- Investing in infrastructure to support the production of healthier foods

- Giving incentives for retailers to sell healthy food in low-income areas

- Setting regulations for preventing unhealthy food outlets in areas where children congregate

- Redesigning the food choices available at the point of sale and making those choices healthier

- Subsidizing healthy foods to increase availability and affordability

- Providing much greater and farther-reaching education on healthy eating and healthy, active living to reduce the disparity and inequities among communities

A Time to Change Successfully

Various factors contribute to the obesity epidemic. Many of the bad habits we all have are a result of the poor choices that we make individually; however, what is considered less often are the cultural forces that are out of our control. In recognizing the forces in the layers of causality, we each can develop our own determination to fight back. As concerned citizens, parents, or professionals, we must dictate change. Public demand still drives this economy; therefore, the more we work toward having a healthy culture and not one that supports and perpetuates unhealthy behaviors that often lead to obesity, the sooner things will get easier for all of us. During the adolescent stage, our teens suffer the most and have a greater potential of experiencing irreversible harm. Promoting positive change in our society makes healthy, active lifestyle choices easier choices to make.

Remember that when your teen decides he or she is ready to make healthy lifestyle changes, they should be lifetime goals, or sustainable efforts that will follow him or her forever. It will take time to change successfully. As long as we continue our forward progress, one foot in front of the other, we will eventually arrive at the finish line. And there is no feeling in the world quite like that!

Resources

. . . .

Alliance for a Healthier Generation. Get informed. **https://www. healthiergeneration.org/about_childhood_obesity/get_informed**. Accessed May 8, 2018

American Academy of Pediatrics. Family media plan. HealthyChildren. org Web site. **https://www.healthychildren.org/MediaUsePlan**. Accessed May 8, 2018

American Academy of Pediatrics. The AAP and The Obesity Society address the social and emotional impact of weight stigma on children and teens. HealthyChildren.org Web site. **https://www.healthychildren. org/English/news/Pages/AAP-ObesitySociety-Impact-Weight-Stigma. aspx**. Published November 20, 2017. Accessed May 8, 2018

Aspen Institute Project Play. *Sport for All, Play for Life: A Playbook to Get Every Kid in the Game.* Washington, DC: Aspen Institute; 2015:18. **https://assets.aspeninstitute.org/content/uploads/2015/01/ Aspen-Institute-Project-Play-Report.pdf**. Accessed May 8, 2018

Centers for Disease Control and Prevention. Adolescents and school health. Whole school, whole community, whole child. **https://www.cdc. gov/healthyyouth/wscc**. Updated March 1, 2018. Accessed May 8, 2018

Centers for Disease Control and Prevention. Healthy schools. Physical education and physical activity. **http://www.cdc.gov/healthyschools/ physicalactivity/index.htm**. Updated January 18, 2018. Accessed May 8, 2018

Centers for Disease Control and Prevention. Overweight & obesity. **https://www.cdc.gov/obesity**. Updated November 29, 2017. Accessed May 8, 2018

Harvard University, TH Chan School of Public Health. The nutrition source. Vegetables and fruits. **http://www.hsph.harvard.edu/ nutritionsource/what-should-you-eat/vegetables-and-fruits**. Accessed May 8, 2018

National Center for Chronic Disease Prevention and Health Promotion Division of Nutrition and Physical Activity. Can eating fruits and vegetables help people to manage their weight? Research to Practice Series, No. 1. **https://www.cdc.gov/nccdphp/dnpa/nutrition/pdf/rtp_practitioner_10_07.pdf**. Accessed May 8, 2018

National Center for Chronic Disease Prevention and Health Promotion, Division of Nutrition, Physical Activity, and Obesity. State initiatives supporting healthier food retail: an overview of the national landscape. **https://www.cdc.gov/obesity/downloads/healthier_food_retail.pdf**. Accessed May 8, 2018

National Center for Safe Routes to School. *Bicycling to School Together: A Bike Train Planning Guide.* Chapel Hill, NC: National Center for Safe Routes to School. **http://www.walkbiketoschool.org/wp-content/uploads/2017/01/SRTS_BikeTrain_final.pdf**. Accessed May 8, 2018

National Farm to School Network. **http://www.farmtoschool.org**. Accessed May 8, 2018

National Physical Activity Plan Alliance. *The 2016 United States Report Card on Physical Activity for Children and Youth.* Columbia, SC; National Physical Activity Plan Alliance; 2016. **http://www.physicalactivityplan.org/reportcard/2016FINAL_USReportCard.pdf**. Accessed May 8, 2018

Office of Disease Prevention and Health Promotion. Chapter 3: active children and adolescents. **https://health.gov/paguidelines/guidelines/chapter3.aspx**. Accessed May 8, 2018

Presidential Youth Fitness Program. **https://www.pyfp.org/get-training/best-practices**. Accessed May 8, 2018

Ripley A. Can teenage defiance be manipulated for good? *The New York Times.* **https://www.nytimes.com/2016/09/13/upshot/can-teenage-defiance-be-manipulated-for-good.html?_r=0**. Published September 12, 2016. Accessed May 8, 2018

US Department of Agriculture Food and Nutrition Service. School meals. Child nutrition programs. **https://www.fns.usda.gov/school-meals/ child-nutrition-programs**. Published May 5, 2018. Accessed May 8, 2018

US Department of Agriculture Food and Nutrition Service. School meals. Tools for schools: focusing on smart snacks. **http://www.fns.usda.gov/ school-meals/smart-snacks-school**. Published November 28, 2017. Accessed May 8, 2018

US Department of Health and Human Services. *2008 Physical Activity Guidelines for Americans.* Washington, DC: US Department of Health and Human Services; 2008. **https://health.gov/paguidelines/pdf/ paguide.pdf**. Accessed May 8, 2018

CHAPTER 8

Living With a Chronic Condition

Parents often begin parenthood feeling that life can't be any harder than those first few weeks with a newborn. With all the challenges that come with caring and raising a healthy baby, what is it like to care for a baby with special needs every day? For parents of children with serious health needs, the difficulties are multiplied.

> I clearly remember the first time I gave my oldest son a bath. It took more than an hour! He weighed a little more than 7 pounds and wasn't longer than 20 inches. To this day I can't tell you what took me so long to bathe him, but I still recall thinking that nothing that I learned in medical school or in residency had prepared me for this and there would probably be many harder times ahead.
>
> I've watched many families battle the challenges emotionally, financially, and logistically to raise a child—and occasionally more than one—who is chronically ill. I am completely and utterly humbled by the way in which so many parents have been able to rise to the occasion, sometimes despite significant financial hardships, and create a sanctuary of love and peace for their child.

Life moves forward for all of us, and puberty doesn't spare children with special needs. As it does for us all, bodily changes, hormone fluctuations, and emotional roller-coaster rides become a reality, even for parents with a special needs child.

Chronic Conditions in Adolescents

It is estimated that approximately 2 million adolescents, equal to approximately 6% of the population between ages 10 and 18 years, have some form of chronic illness that affects them on a daily basis or causes a disability. When an adolescent has a chronic health condition, it potentially places an additional physical and psychological burden on an already challenging period. The most common of these chronic health conditions are asthma and other chronic respiratory tract diseases, musculoskeletal disorders, and heart disease.

Puberty and Chronic Illness

Chapters 1 and 4 discussed the physical and emotional growth that takes place in children during puberty. Children who live with a chronic condition often experience the changes of puberty differently than their unaffected peers. This places added stress on the teen during the process of puberty, which already carries enough physical and emotional challenges for the average child or teen without a chronic health condition.

The following are some of the chronic conditions that consistently interfere with puberty:

- **Inflammatory bowel disease (IBD):** Because of the malabsorption and chronic inflammation that are characteristic of these disorders, illnesses such as ulcerative colitis and Crohn disease (commonly referred to as Crohn's disease) often are associated with growth delay and delay of puberty.

- **Cystic fibrosis (CF):** Growth and puberty are delayed in children with CF also because of malabsorption and chronic inflammation.

- **Renal and liver disease:** The excess toxins and inflammation that are produced with these illnesses affect growth and puberty.

- **Diabetes (type 1):** The harmful effects of hyperglycemia are the primary causes for delay of growth and puberty in children with diabetes.

- **Celiac disease:** An autoimmune disorder that is triggered by eating products with gluten, such as wheat, barley, rye, and other grains; can cause delays and interfere with normal growth and puberty.

Psychological Adjustment

During my residency training, I met dozens of patients with inflammatory bowel disease (IBD) and their families, all of whom had to negotiate puberty and this debilitating chronic disease. There was no question that the average male patient living with IBD that I interacted with was very small and immature looking for his stated age. When examined, the patient consistently had delayed puberty that resulted in reciprocal effects on development. Given how young these teens looked, it was easy to forget their actual age and interact with them as if they were much younger.

The patients' friends and families also may behave this way with them. As a group, the patients were likely to show little initiative in taking an active role in their own care; in addition, their parents were likely to be very overprotective. Low self-esteem was common, and difficulties with psychological adjustments accompanied this diagnosis so consistently that our department employed a full-time child psychiatrist to work with these teens and their families.

Delayed Puberty

Frequently, the delay in growth and puberty seen in patients with chronic conditions is short-lived, and they will catch up later. The speed of the growth spurt will be delayed in more than 50% of kids living with IBD, and 25% will show very significant short stature in adolescence. Teens living with IBD should receive specialized care that regularly monitors progression of height, weight, and body mass index to determine if a growth spurt and pubertal development have begun. These developmental factors can continue to be followed up on as needed to ensure that the delays are addressed as best as possible.

In a 5-year study of teens living with type 1 diabetes, 86 teens with diabetes were compared to 103 healthy controls. In the first year of the study, the teens with diabetes reported delays in some developmental tasks, particularly physical maturity and an independent lifestyle, compared with their healthy peers. However, these delays had resolved by the end of the study. Approximately 1 year of pubertal onset delay is common when the teen's type 1 diabetes is poorly controlled. This delay is frequently accompanied by short-lived delay of growth in early adolescence. The patient's average final height, though, is normal in many populations with type 1 diabetes.

The Effects of Chronic Illness on Cognitive and Emotional Development

Puberty is packed with enormous developmental transformations in the physical, emotional, and intellectual capabilities of a child emerging into adulthood. A chronic condition might have a profound effect on puberty; likewise, it is reasonable to consider that puberty may change the way the chronic condition behaves. There are many things to consider.

Emotional Effects

Some studies of teens living with chronic conditions reveal that adolescent girls with a chronic condition were more likely to have emotional problems than their healthy counterparts; however, the same was not true for boys. Also, research shows that teens with a chronic condition might have a higher prevalence of at least one psychiatric diagnosis, such as depression, compared to healthy teens. Adolescents with type 1 diabetes appear to be as psychologically well-adjusted as their healthy peers, whereas adolescents living with asthma show more symptoms of sadness, loneliness, depression, and physical issues than their healthy peers.

Cognitive Effects

Chronic illness during puberty probably does not affect the basic way in which the brain rearranges itself as it develops abstract thinking skills. Certain chronic conditions, however, such as type 1 diabetes and sickle cell disease, are known to have long-term neuropsychological effects in adolescents. In those with type 1 diabetes, this is attributed to the effects of hypoglycemia, and in those with sickle cell disease, it is thought to be a result of blood vessel damage in the brain. These effects are not suspected to be the result of the general state of having a chronic condition. In contrast, there is evidence that identity, self-image, and ego development are affected by chronic conditions in a generic fashion. This is particularly true when illness is more severe and IQ is higher.

Body Image

Body image and the development of sensuality may be impaired by chronic conditions because of distortions of the physical body, such as scars or stomas (openings made in the body such as a tracheotomy that assists with breathing or a colostomy that allows feces to bypass the intestines and flow into a bag). Required treatments such as occasional removal of a prosthetic eye may be very off-putting to others. Population-based studies show that adolescents with a chronic condition report higher body dissatisfaction than adolescents with no chronic condition. These body image issues focus particularly on weight but are not limited to conditions that are typically nutrition related, such as type 1 diabetes. These issues result in higher rates of high-risk weight-loss practices. Body image issues or dissatisfaction theoretically may impair later sexual function, although population-based studies suggest that adolescents with a chronic condition have higher rates of sexual intercourse and unsafe sexual practices than healthy controls. Body image problems possibly may act to increase risky sexual behavior.

Caring for adolescents with obstacles to puberty such as those discussed here is a huge challenge. It is difficult to know how to best help them with their physical issues and any emotional challenges. Their issues include all the typical things that occur with puberty as well as the specifics of their illness, both in general and in relation to puberty. It can be very difficult for parents to find successful approaches for navigating development in a healthy and positive way when chronic illness complicates growth.

Ways for Parents to Find Strength

Put on your own oxygen mask first. You are of little use to your teen living with a chronic condition if you are unhealthy. Concentrate on all the elements of health and well-being for yourself; many of these important considerations can be found in Chapter 10. Although Chapter 10 is written with the adolescent in mind, some principles discussed have no age limit. Model the lifestyle that you want your teen to emulate.

Let go of the things you cannot change. This is easy to say, especially if you are not a parent raising a teen with medical problems, but it doesn't change the fact that you cannot change what is; you can only change your attitude. There is a great quote that says, "A bad attitude is like a flat tire; you can't go anywhere until you fix it!" Hard as it might be to see what you have to be thankful for, you will feel better if you can find the strength to believe that. Give yourself permission to let go of your visions of unattainable family perfection.

Share the burden with others who relate. Join a support group, or even start a support group. At first, you may have reservations about how useful this can be, but never doubt the value of empathy, compassion, and support from others.

Consider talking to a mental health professional. Under normal circumstances, seeking help from a qualified mental health professional can be incredibly cathartic. When you are trying to navigate the world with a sick child, it can be life-altering for you. If you feel that you have lost your ability to cope or function daily in a healthy way, seek out help for yourself. It can be a game changer.

Find your silver lining. It is possible that your life and the life of your child may be better in some way because of the chronic condition. Some examples include not sweating the small stuff, being less judgmental and having more compassion for strangers, worrying less about achieving perfection in life, dwelling less on things out of your control, laughing more and not taking things too seriously, having a positive attitude, and taking better care of your health and others. If you are able to envision how this might be true for you and your family, it can have a freeing effect on your household.

For parents struggling to figure out a strategy for navigating puberty for a child with a chronic condition, here are a collection of tips. Hopefully, you will discover some ideas in this list that resonate with you.

Tips for Parents to Help Their Teens

Stop Rescuing Your Teen

For years you have been "popping in" whenever your teen has a health issue. Your teen is growing up and, like all teens, needs to learn how to be independent. Try to allow your teen to solve the situation on his or her own. You might be surprised at how capable your teen is; however, if your teen is not yet able to handle the situation alone, use each situation as a teachable moment. Your teen will get there.

View the Glass as Half Full

Don't succumb to a "woe is me" attitude. No one wants to be defined by an illness. Don't allow that attitude in yourself or your teen. Always use "people-first" language. For example, an individual with diabetes should not be called a diabetic, but rather a teenager living with diabetes.

Consider the Alternative

The next time you are making a decision for your preteen or teen about something weighty, stop for a second and ask yourself, "If my son didn't have Crohn's disease, would I let him go on the trip?" If the answer is yes, I would advise you to really stop and think about why you want to say no. Is your teen ready to manage medications and issues yet? How far away is your teen going for college? How will your teen have the tools to go to college if he or she is not given or doesn't accept any personal responsibility now? Can you sit with your teen and review the details of what it would take to go away with friends? Could you discuss contingency plans? You might be frightened to death, but this is doable. Your teen may feel like a different person if allowed to go.

Discuss Scenarios Calmly

Imagine your teen has a severe allergy to bees and wants to go on an overnight school camping trip with friends. You want your teen to go, but you are terrified of a possible bee sting and the need for an epinephrine autoinjector (eg, EpiPen) without you there. Calmly and without stress, discuss with your teen some "what if" scenarios in the event of a bee sting. Help your teen have the confidence that he or she can manage this lifesaving scenario without you being there. Practice what should be told in advance to friends, reiterate how the epinephrine autoinjector should be kept handy at all times, make sure that your teen knows how to use it, and advise your teen that a friend or an adult may need to apply it if your teen is unable to. This discussion provides necessary information for your teen, and it will help you both know that he or she is taking responsibility and can be trusted with his or her own health.

Educational Challenges

There are many educational challenges when a child or teen has a chronic condition. Depending on the specific medical problem, the child or teen may require specialized services or accommodations. Greater than average school absences are probable. Interestingly, young people living with chronic health issues miss more school days than their peers because of their health problems and also because they are more likely to skip school. In fact, adolescents with chronic health conditions often miss school days that cannot be attributed to their treatment needs. Pediatricians can assist families in coordinating their adolescent's health care and partnering with the school and its district committee on special education.

Special Accommodations

I am a practicing pediatrician in general pediatrics, but, I am also a New York State Trainer for Child Abuse and Neglect and the school physician for many Nassau County public schools. As a school physician, it is my responsibility to review and approve accommodations for services, such as transportation. When a child breaks a leg, it is easy to approve a request for 6 to 8 weeks of door-to-door bus transportation. But what about the 13-year-old living with asthma whose parent wants door-to-door transportation because the asthma may flare up in the cold weather? And what about the 15-year-old with a seizure disorder who hasn't had a seizure in more than a year? Does this teen need door-to-door transportation? Does the 12-year-old with newly diagnosed type 1 diabetes need a one-to-one aide to follow him or her around school to make sure that the child properly checks glucose levels? Does the child need an aide to help recognize signs of hypoglycemia, or can the school nurse, or even the tween, do that?

To determine the answers to these questions, I must review the general physical and school medical histories of each adolescent. I need to know specifically what problems the adolescent has had that corroborate that his or her health is in jeopardy without the requested service. In the case of the teen living with asthma, I want to know how many days were lost from school in relation to the asthma or asthma-related problems, how many days the teen spent in the hospital, how many times gym class was missed, what regular medication is prescribed and taken regularly, and how many visits have been made to the school nurse. I have a similar line of questioning about each of these individuals, specific to the condition. The goal of the questioning is to uncover one major point: does this individual have a chronic condition that renders him or her so fragile that taking door-to-door bus transportation will benefit him or her more than having as typical an adolescent school experience as possible? For those families who are genuinely scared about their adolescent with a chronic condition, it is my responsibility to know whether this request is in the adolescent's overall medical and psychological best interest. During puberty, when self-esteem is especially fragile, it is critical to consider the risk and benefit of some services. I always remind myself that I never want to enable an adolescent already dealing with a respiratory, cardiac, neurologic, or other chronic condition to be consumed by his or her illness and handicapped unnecessarily. Allowing adolescents with chronic conditions to have as typical an existence as their illness permits is a priority.

Family and Peer Challenges

At a time when most parents are feeling relief from the part of puberty in which they are constantly policing activities of daily living, such as making sure the adolescent's teeth are brushed, a chronic condition creates great challenges for parents and teens. Other kids may be running off with their peers at every possible moment, but a teen with spina bifida who is wheelchair bound most likely is not able to do that. Parents still need to encourage that teen to engage in being as typical a teenager as possible. Every effort should be made to allow an adolescent with a chronic condition to have strong peer relationships. Research shows that many young people with chronic conditions report having excellent peer relationships, and there is evidence that an illness such as cancer may even increase peer acceptability.

The Effects of Puberty on the Management of Chronic Conditions

During puberty adolescents may not wish to comply with the treatment plan that has been in place and managed predominantly by their parents. They now are at an age at which they insist on some independence, but they may appear ill-prepared to take on the responsibility. When abstract thinking is developing but not yet complete, a teen won't consider or thoroughly think through situations; neglects to consider the consequences of noncompliance, especially long term; and has a relatively poor ability to plan and prepare for different situations using abstract concepts. The teen may consider himself or herself to be invincible, as many teens do, and imagine that the rules of life apply to everyone else but him or her. Additionally, the teen may disagree with the health care beliefs and goals of his or her health care professionals or family.

Peer relationships and self-image evolve during puberty. What clothes to wear, how to behave in public, and what gets posted on social media become more and more of a priority. These priorities may be in direct conflict with the demands of treatment or regimens of care for the chronically ill teen or for one with specific orthopedic, neuromuscular, or other disabilities. The extent to which adolescent issues affect illness management and control depends on how the teen can balance these competing priorities. Middle adolescence is intensely associated with the need to establish an identity. This is indicated by teens' keen interest in peer activities and sometimes even in rebellious attitudes. Many adolescents with chronic conditions may feel too tightly controlled and may ask for more freedom in managing their condition. The relationship with the health care team, even in previously smooth instances marked by mutual respect, may be abruptly shattered by an attempt to gain independence.

Managing Asthma

Asthma is one of the most common chronic conditions affecting kids in the United States. Years ago, treating asthma was much more cumbersome. Treatment options such as inhaled corticosteroid medications, which can keep significant asthma in control and are nearly without significant side effects, were not yet available. These inhalers eliminated the need for a bulky and time-consuming nebulizer for treating an acute asthma attack. Instead the teen uses a small rescue inhaler with a spacer. A spacer usually consists of a cylindrical tube that attaches to the inhaler. The purpose of the spacer is to ensure that the inhaled medication is delivered properly to the lungs and not predominantly to the back of the tongue, which is typically what would happen without the spacer. Controller inhalers are taken at fixed times, making it easy to have a spacer available to use. Using a spacer for controllers that are not breath-actuated is a must for proper delivery of controller medications daily to prevent attacks.

A rescue inhaler is used for sudden difficulties with breathing and must be carried by your teen at all times. It is small and fits in a pocket, backpack, or purse. A spacer will fit in a backpack but not a pocket or a purse. Often, teens express to me that they do not carry a spacer, and I approach this in a way that meets the teen's needs and is medically appropriate. Some of these approaches include having a discussion about using a controller medication that doesn't require a spacer, or ensuring that spacers are available in situations where rescue medication might be more likely to be needed, such as when participating in sports. It is always understood that if a teen's ability to control asthma becomes a concern, we will have to readdress this.

Risk-taking Behavior

Typical adolescent risk-taking behavior, although anticipated, is quite unwelcome and results from impulsiveness, the rejection of parental values, the testing of boundaries, and a larger dopamine response. We know that a connection with strong family, community, and school support can protect against most health-risk behaviors in adolescents. Identifying such protective factors (or resilience) is the focus of many public health interventions with adolescents. The search for protective factors applies equally to the management of chronic conditions throughout puberty.

Resilience Strategies for Parents

Parents can try the following strategies aimed toward developing teen resilience, although not all ideas are appropriate for every teen. In general, the goal is for their teen to become self-sufficient and feel comfortable managing his or her own health issues.

- Help your teen have a good and trusting relationship with his or her pediatrician. Pediatricians can offer invaluable education and support.

- Practice strategies to help your teen discuss his or her illness with others by having him or her do the following:

  - Prepare and practice delivery of an educational speech about his or her condition.

  - Talk about how the condition affects him or her day to day.

  - Have friends and others ask questions.

  - Prepare something for people to read about the condition.

  - Encourage sensitivity to cues from others.

  - Encourage the teen to not overwhelm others with information but, rather, provide as much information as others seem interested in hearing about or able to take in at the time.

  - Support your teen in making and having close peer relationships.

- Consider encouraging your teen to be a volunteer. Helping others is a great way to take the focus off of one's own health problems and build empathy.

■ Encourage structure in your teen's daily routine. This might be tough but would be useful.

■ Help your teen care for himself or herself by encouraging independence as much as possible.

■ Help your teen to see that the ability to deal with his or her chronic condition is a shining example of strength.

■ Resist the urge to rescue your teen at every opportunity. Teens need to develop competency to feel good about themselves.

■ Help your teen to view puberty as the wonderful period of great change that it is. Your teen will be OK and so will you!

A Plan for Independence

Your child, your joy and your world, is living life with a chronic condition. Until now, it was entirely up to you to plan how things got done. You no longer had to worry once you figured out your plan. Now your adolescent has entered puberty and has other ideas about managing the chronic condition, and those ideas usually involve ignoring it. You are at your wit's end with how to survive the transition through puberty with an adolescent who is chronically ill. You're thrilled that he or she is doing what all the other kids are doing but with one big exception—your adolescent needs to attend to his or her medical needs to stay healthy. What are parents to do? The rules are the same for you as with a parent whose child does not have a chronic condition, but the stakes are a lot higher. The key to success with an adolescent going through puberty is to be supportive, open, and nonjudgmental. You need to give your adolescent the space needed to gain confidence and successful independence and help him or her develop resilience. This is never more apparent than it is for parents of an adolescent with a chronic condition. As counterintuitive as it may sound, teens living with a chronic condition will be the hardest ones to let go of, but there is no one who needs to fly more.

Amy's Story

I first met 1-month-old Amy when I was a first-year pediatric resident. She had exceptionally yellow skin, medically referred to as jaundice. Newborn jaundice is easily treatable with lights or goes away on its own. But Amy did not have newborn jaundice.

Diagnosis

Amy's jaundice resulted from a very serious liver condition that required surgery. If the surgery proved successful, she could have 20 years or more of quality living before she would require a liver transplant.

Amy was one of my first patients in my career as a pediatrician, and her case was complicated and heartbreaking. Her mother and I developed a close relationship. The surgery went well, though Amy spent the years that I was going through residency as a "frequent flyer": she had medical problems related to her diagnosis that necessitated numerous hospital admissions.

After completing my residency and joining a private practice, I was thrilled to discover that Amy was a general patient of mine. As Amy grew, it was clear that she would need a liver transplant before reaching puberty, a lot earlier than doctors had originally hoped. By age 6 years, her complexion was very jaundiced, almost a fluorescent shade of yellow-green. Her belly was swollen due to her enlarged, failing liver.

New Hurdles

Amy received a liver transplant at Children's Hospital of Philadelphia (CHOP). She was no longer fluorescent green, and her liver was no longer enlarged. Her biggest health hurdles consisted of taking her daily pre-scribed medication, which prevented the rejection of her new liver, and monthly blood work to confirm that the liver was healthy. She also had to consistently see the transplant team at CHOP and her gastrointestinal team locally for routine care.

One day when Amy was in her early teens, we were reviewing her routine blood work and her liver enzyme results came back as abnormal. The transplant team advised me to start her on a course of steroids and recheck her blood work. Fortunately, this brought her enzymes back to a normal level. However, 6 months later, we again received abnormal enzyme results and I was again advised to prescribe steroids. Various thoughts flooded my mind: Could this liver be failing? Would she need another transplant? Why was this happening?

There was a huge amount of concern surrounding the cause of Amy's liver problems. Everything seemed to occur randomly without any obvious trigger. The CHOP team suggested that we consider the possibility that Amy might not be taking her medication properly. They advised that we carefully determine if the pill count was correct. Amy's mother admitted that she had recently begun to trust Amy with the responsibility of taking her own medicine. This was something she would have to manage successfully for the remainder of her life, so as a young teen, it seemed the proper time to give her that responsibility. The pills were counted, and we quickly received our answer. The lifesaving medicine that Amy needed to take daily was either purposely not being taken, or she was missing many doses.

The Hard Truth

Amy admitted that she was not taking her medication diligently. Skipping her medication was sending her liver into rejection. The steroids that we administered each time her enzyme results were off were capable of rescuing the situation. But why was this happening? You may suspect that Amy had problems with depression, anxiety, or her self-image. She was an emerging teen with an abdomen ravaged by lifesaving surgery. But it wasn't any of those things. It turns out that Amy didn't feel like taking her medications on a daily basis anymore. She had often told me that she remembered next to nothing about her condition before her liver transplant even though she had often heard about how sick she had been and how close she had come to dying. Once Amy realized and accepted the seriousness of her decision to stop taking her medication, she immediately resumed responsibility of her health. Today, she is a successful social worker with a beautiful daughter!

To work with adolescents, especially when a chronic condition complicates the situation, pediatricians and sometimes even parents must think like adolescents to have any meaningful effect. Rational decisions require abstract thinking, and even then, one might fall short of achieving the most rational answers. But rational thought is not yet a part of the younger adolescent's equation. When adolescents travel through puberty with a chronic condition, some of the aspects of adolescence may manifest themselves in very dangerous ways that can create life-and-death situations, even though they are entirely self-imposed. I share Amy's story because it could easily have pertained to thousands of other kids with a chronic condition.

Resources

American Academy of Pediatrics. *ADHD: What Every Parent Needs to Know.* Reiff MI, ed. 2nd ed. Elk Grove Village, IL: American Academy of Pediatrics; 2011

American Academy of Pediatrics. *Autism Spectrum Disorders: What Every Parent Needs to Know.* Rosenblatt AI, Carbone PS, eds. Elk Grove Village, IL: American Academy of Pediatrics; 2013

CHAPTER 9

The Effects of Puberty on Exercise and Sports Performance

Promoting physical literacy is every bit as important as basic literacy. Physical literacy is the ability, confidence, and desire to be physically active for life. Many studies conclusively show that exercise and activity are instrumental in improving children's focus, memory, and cognitive ability for specific subjects such as mathematics.

Having higher aerobic fitness helps with focus and attention. When children are challenged with specific tasks that require a great deal of concentration, attention, and focus, those with higher aerobic fitness levels perform better in both accuracy and reaction time. For example, in a study of reaction times, children were asked to quickly identify pictures of items such as animals, answering questions like, "Is it a dog or a cat?" The kids who were more fit had better reaction times and accuracy.

Children who are more fit may retain information longer. In a study of groups of kids who memorized areas on a map, the children who were more fit showed better retention of the information from the day before when they were retested the next day. Their degree of fitness was determined using a maximal oxygen consumption test completed on a motorized treadmill.

Effect of Exercise on Performance

Performance was improved in children who ordinarily performed poorly on tasks associated with attention when they were tested shortly after being given a small boost of exercise consisting of a 20-minute walk on a treadmill. A study was conducted with a group of 56 kids placed into 1 of 3 groups: those who sat all morning; those who did 90 minutes of schoolwork and then were given a 20-minute exercise break; and those who did 20 minutes of exercise, followed by 90 minutes of schoolwork, and then another 20 minutes of exercise.

Results showed that the group with the 2 exercise breaks performed better during tests for attention. A randomized study showed that after 13 weeks of exercise, children's math skills were better. Exercise sessions that consisted of 20 minutes of walking boosted performance on reading, spelling, and arithmetic tests.

Finally, in a study of second and third graders in the Netherlands that looked at whether adding physical activity could help children improve their math and spelling, children were placed into 1 of 2 groups. One group continued with standard lessons, while the other group participated in a series of lessons in which physical exercise was used when teaching math and language. After 2 years, the children participating in the active learning group had significant improvements in math and spelling standardized test scores as compared with children in the group that continued with standard lessons, demonstrating that physically active teaching lessons show promise as a new teaching method. Although this study was conducted with young children, the results have implications for all ages.

This chapter will look at sports participation during puberty via several different angles. We will discuss the general state of athletics in the United States today, physical literacy, and the role physical literacy plays in influencing overall health and well-being. We will look at the typical selection process in sports, why children are leaving sports, how the process of puberty directly affects performance, considerations when choosing a sport during puberty, and sports specialization.

The Current State of Athletics in the United States

The nation, concerned parents, schools, and health care professionals share a goal of wanting to support the success of our children and identify the best and most effective ways to do that. Understanding physical literacy is an important step toward affecting the future successes of our children.

According to a poll from the National Alliance for Youth Sports, approximately 70% of kids in the United States will drop out of organized sports by age 13 years, saying that sports are no longer fun. Clearly, the current methods of running youth sports programs are not encouraging kids to join or stay in the programs. Rethinking how we promote athletics has important implications for the future health and wellness of our children and, ultimately, our nation.

The Process of Selection for Sports Teams

When we look at the process of selecting children for different sports in the United States, we see a system that tries to find and promote the most talented children. Identifying talented and potential athletic stars begins with very young children and is a flawed process.

Age

Selecting children for sports teams is supposedly based on talent, but because the groupings are usually done by chronological age and not by developmental ability, the children who are born in the first 3 months of the calendar year are typically the ones who demonstrate the most talent. Their talent is a function of their physical maturity, which correlates with their age and has very little to do with actual talent.

Maturity

Sports teams often will hold tryouts to determine who is selected. In these tryouts, children are selected more for chronological maturity than for athletic talent. In addition, the judges at such tryouts are not independent highly skilled evaluators. When all-star teams are selected by these types of methods and children who have not yet reached puberty are cut, we cheat ourselves out of the opportunity to discover players with future potential. What we actually are doing is selecting players who are a bit older, more physically mature, and more skilled than those who were cut from play.

This selection model results in many children being discouraged from play before they even have a chance to perform. Not only do we rob ourselves of potential talent, but we discourage leagues of children who are now sitting out and considering themselves athletic failures before they even had a chance to try.

Physical Literacy and Sports

The fact that many children drop out from or never even begin participating in athletics has great repercussions for societal health and well-being. Today, we are looking at a population of children that is dominated by obesity (see Chapter 7). These children might be the first generation to have a shorter life span than their parents.

Creating and building a culture that values and promotes a love and appreciation of physical activity is a lofty goal that has the potential to have an enormous positive effect on the future health and wellness of our nation. All children should be involved, regardless of socioeconomic factors, athletic abilities, and disabilities. Many concerned organizations currently are working tirelessly to bring about such change.

Too many children are choosing not to continue playing through puberty. An active lifestyle is crucial to health and wellness and sports participation is one way to establish the habits and skills that active people have. When asked why they no longer want to participate in sports, children say that a lack of fun is the main reason for leaving sports. If lack of enjoyment is cited as the main reason children no longer wish to participate in organized sports, it certainly seems prudent to try to uncover what "fun" truly means to them and seek ways to rectify the problem. In a book published by Routledge titled *Sport Psychology for Young Athletes*, a research team used concept mapping to ask and analyze data from youth, parents, and soccer coaches to answer the question, "What makes sports fun?" "Fun" ideas were contributed through qualitative brainstorming, identifying all the things that make playing sports fun for players; sorting of ideas; and rating each idea on its importance, frequency, and feasibility. Eleven fun-factors and 81 determinants were identified as the determinants of fun (Box 9-1).

Box 9-1. The Determinants of Fun

One thing that makes playing sports fun for players is...

Trying Hard
- Trying your best
- Working hard
- Exercising and being active
- Getting/staying in shape
- Playing well during a game
- Being strong and confident
- Competing
- Making a good play (scoring, big save, etc)
- Setting and achieving goals
- Playing hard

Positive Team Dynamics
- Playing well together as a team
- Supporting my teammates
- When players show good sportspersonship
- Being supported by my teammates
- Getting help from teammates
- Warming up and stretching as a team

Learning and Improving
- Being challenged to improve/get better
- Learning from mistakes
- Improving athletic skills to play at the next level
- Ball touches (dribbling, passing, shooting, etc)
- Learning new skills
- Using a skill learned in practice during a game
- Playing different positions
- Going to sports camp
- Copying moves and tricks of pro athletes

Games
- Getting playing time
- Playing your favorite position
- Playing against an evenly matched team
- Being known by others for your sport skills
- Playing on a nice field
- Playing in tournaments

Mental Bonuses
- Keeping a positive attitude
- Winning
- It relieves stress
- Ignoring the score

Game Time Support
- A ref who makes consistent calls
- Parents showing good sportspersonship (encouraging)
- Being congratulated for playing well
- Having people cheer at the game
- Having your parent(s) watch your games
- Getting complimented by other parents

Team Rituals
- Showing team spirit with gear, ribbons, signs, etc
- High-fiving, fist-bumping, hugging
- End-of-season/team parties

Box 9-1. The Determinants of Fun (*continued*)

One thing that makes playing sports fun for players is...

Positive Coaching

- When a coach treats players with respect
- A coach who knows a lot about the sport
- Having a coach who is a positive role model
- When a coach encourages the team
- Clear, consistent communication from coach
- A coach who listens and considers players' opinions
- A coach who allows mistakes, while staying positive
- A coach who you can talk to easily
- A nice, friendly coach
- Getting compliments from coaches
- When a coach participates during practice
- When a coach jokes around

Practice

- Having well-organized practices
- Taking water breaks during practice
- Having the freedom to play creatively
- Doing lots of different drills/activities in practice
- Scrimmaging during practice
- Partner and small group drills
- Practicing with specialty trainers/coaches

Team Friendships

- Getting along with your teammates
- Being around your friends
- Having a group of friends outside of school
- Hanging with teammates outside practice, games
- Being part of the same team year after year
- Meeting new people
- Talking and goofing off with teammates
- Going out to eat as a team
- Doing team rituals
- Carpooling with teammates to practices/games
- Doing a cool team cheer

Swag

- Having nice sports gear and equipment
- Earning medals or trophies
- Traveling to new places to play
- Wearing a special, cool uniform
- Eating snacks/treats after the game
- Staying in hotels for games/tournaments
- Getting pictures taken

Source: Visek et al, in *Sport Psychology for Young Athletes,* Knight et al, Copyright © 2018 and Routledge, reproduced by permission of Taylor & Francis Books UK.

When fully analyzed, "being a good sport," "trying hard," and "positive coaching" were 3 of the 11 fun-factors determined, followed by "learning and improving," "games," "practices," "team friendships," "mental bonuses," "team rituals," "game time support," and "swag." Rethinking our strategies in developing sports programs for children and adolescents to address the concept of physical literacy, as well as what kids consider to be fun, may be long overdue. What kids consider to be fun must be regarded as well.

Fun Integration Theory

The results of the "fun" study identify and create a framework known as the fun integration theory, or FIT, which parents, coaches, and players can use to better identify what really matters when it comes to creating a fun sports experience. One in 3 children is considered to have an unhealthy weight, so this research offers much hope in promoting legitimate fun with the promise of more kids participating for a longer time in sports. This can lead to better emotional, social, and cognitive abilities for these kids.

How else is this information useful to parents? If you wish to know whether your child should play football, you should investigate the coaching strategies of the program in which he or she is interested. Identify whether the main characteristics of the program are in line with the information uncovered by the "fun" research. This should help you determine whether joining a particular program would be a successful experience for your child. Having a fun experience will go a very long way in keeping your child physically strong, academically and socially successful, and, ultimately, happy and healthy.

Pubertal Development and Adolescent Growth Spurt

Puberty affects adolescents' physical activities by affecting their physical growth and emotional status, as well as the way they develop muscularly. These changes should be taken into consideration in any sports activities.

Physical Effects

Pubertal development influences your adolescent's sports performance. Coaches and trainers who are well educated on the effects of the adolescent growth spurt understand how this somewhat unbalanced growth can affect their athletes and can adjust their coaching and training plans accordingly. During peak growth, boys can grow as much as 4 inches in a year, whereas girls tend to grow up to 2½ inches. Athletic performance can be affected in positive and negative ways. Adolescents will have increased body size and developing muscles, which may improve athletic performance, but balancing skills and body control may temporarily decline. A certain degree of awkwardness may appear because growth is occurring so rapidly. Quick increases in height and weight affect the body's center of gravity. Sometimes, the brain has to adjust to this higher observation point, and a teen may seem a bit clumsy.

This phase is especially noticeable in sports that require good balance and body control, such as figure skating, diving, gymnastics, or basketball. Adolescents who were very coordinated as children may suddenly find themselves less so. In addition, longer arms and legs can affect throwing any type of ball, hitting a ball with a bat or racquet, catching the ball with a glove or lacrosse stick, swimming, and jumping. Pitchers may need help with executing their pitches; batters may need to adjust the timing of their swing. Coaches and trainers who are aware of the effects of the adolescent growth spurt can help reduce athletic awkwardness by incorporating specific aspects of training into practices and training sessions.

Tips to Stay Athletically Fit During the Adolescent Growth Spurt

One program that addresses the adolescent growth spurt (AGS) and suggests specific training modifications for adolescents during this period is Soccer Speed and Agility Clinic, created by Scott Moody of Soccer Fit Academy. It is written with soccer players in mind, but the concepts are applicable to adolescent athletes of other sports. Five factors, based on sports fundamentals, are stressed for the teen experiencing AGS. During this phase of development, it is especially important to ensure proper biomechanics, which means optimal body movement and positioning, at all times throughout training.

Movement-based strength. This will mostly center on running, squatting, jumping, lunging, pivoting, and rotating. The training goal is to make the movements rhythmic by stressing repetition, to recruit correct patterns of movement, and to develop confidence with movement strength.

Overall fitness. This factor pertains to the level of play that allows the athlete to perform optimally. Sports injuries are less likely with good fitness levels.

Speed and agility. During the adolescent growth spurt, athletes need to relearn how to control their bodies during directional changes, change of pace, and acceleration.

Plyometric work. Also known as "jump training" or "plyos," plyometric work consists of exercises in which muscles exert maximum force in short intervals with the goal of increasing power. This factor is important for explosive strength, speed, and agility, and it can be a part of other areas of training, such as basic strength training.

Confidence. It cannot be stressed enough that the adolescent must be reminded during his or her growth spurt that it is temporary and he or she has not lost ability. Involved adults are well aware of the time-limited nature of these setbacks, but the teen may be incapable of recognizing the transient nature of this period. Instilling a sense of confidence always is critical to success.

During the adolescent growth spurt, it is likely that an adolescent will need to be retrained in movement patterns. The emphasis should be on movement, rhythm, and coordination over strength, fitness, and power. A program that is sensitive to the challenges of rapid growth allows the adolescent to reduce coordination and balance issues, decrease the extent of awkwardness that exists, and achieve his or her best level of sports performance.

Supporting a Temporary Phase

Most of the changes associated with the adolescent growth spurt are temporary. Offer reassurance to your teen such as the following:

- Remind your adolescent often that this is a temporary situation.

- Remind him or her that he or she still has abilities.

- Encourage your adolescent to work on movement, coordination, and rhythm skills to counterbalance the AGS awkwardness.

- Find positive things to say about his or her efforts and present ability.

- Be your adolescent's greatest cheerleader!

Emotional Effects

Parents and coaches should be supportive and understand that a sudden lack of performance might not be because of a lack of effort or interest. Be the voice of reason for your adolescent by telling him or her about the following:

- You have been very competent in your sport, and the difficulties you are experiencing are due to your growth spurt.

- You cannot control having a growth spurt, but you can control how you react to it.

- You can focus on specific training that will help you with the temporary changes that you are going through.

- I believe in and support you.

- The decision to continue to work hard is yours to make.

The Female Adolescent Athlete

Female athletes going through puberty may experience anxiety when beginning to menstruate. When a girl first gets her period, she may become somewhat insecure, especially if her sport is directly affected, such as in swimming or in sports like gymnastics that require uniforms that are difficult to wear confidently when menstruating. Girls may feel terribly self-conscious, most notably if they cannot yet use a tampon. Having a period may interrupt a girl's participation in her sport for several days. Parents can help by being very sensitive to their daughter's possible dilemmas. They can consider options, such as whether she has the maturity to learn how to use a tampon safely to be able to continue participating in her sport without disruption.

Weight Training

Another aspect of the adolescent growth spurt is the development of strength. Before puberty, there is little difference between boys and girls, but as the growth spurt proceeds, girls gain a small amount of muscle and some increased fat. Boys, however, gain about 40 pounds over the course of puberty, most of it muscle. Many boys, and even their parents, ask me about the possibility of promoting muscle development with weight training. Boys often believe that they can influence the development of muscles by beginning a rigorous weight training program. The relationship between the muscles and tendons with the young bone and growth plates creates more risk of injury during this time. It is only once the growth spurt is complete that the muscles will enlarge; prior to AGS, there are not enough of the hormones that are needed to cause significant muscle enlargement.

Weight training performed with light weights and repetition sets and supervised properly by a qualified professional, however, can be a great way to build bone density and balance, but the adolescent must have proper form and technique with a properly matched weight for his or her ability. Combining resistance training with other programs such as neuromuscular training are meant to enhance muscle firing and movement patterns for improvement skills needed for exercise and sports activities. Well-rounded programs include resistance training as one part of the overall training with the ultimate goal of better fitness, strength, and activity levels for youth.

Preventing Injuries

During the adolescent growth spurt, a teen has specific vulnerability to certain injuries. Inside the ends of adolescents' bones is a section of cartilage, called the growth plate, that is responsible for growth and that eventually turns into bone when the adolescent is finished growing. The growth plate is much more delicate than the surrounding bone, muscle, tendons, or ligaments; it is weakest during the adolescent growth spurt. Injury to the growth plate can limit proper growth.

Injuries to the growth plate are fractures. Some growth plate injuries are caused by a fall or a blow to the limb, while others result from over-use or repetitive stress to the growth plate. For example, a gymnast who practices tumbling routines for many hours each week, a long-distance runner ramping up mileage in preparation for a race, or a baseball pitcher perfecting his or her fastball are all at risk for overuse injuries to the growth plate.

The Anterior Cruciate Ligament (ACL) During Puberty

As preteens enter into puberty and grow taller and heavier, their risk of anterior cruciate ligament (ACL) injury increases. The ACL is one of the main ligaments providing stability to the knee. It is 1 of 4 main ligaments inside the knee, running from the femur (thighbone) to the tibia (shinbone). It keeps the tibia from sliding forward on the femur and stabilizes the knee when it rotates or twists. Sports with predominantly forward motion, such as jogging, swimming, and biking, place little stress on the ACL. The ACL plays a vital role in stabilizing the knee in sports such as soccer and basketball, which involve cutting, planting, and changing directions. These sports have a higher risk of ACL injury, and in these sports, females have a higher risk than males.

According to the American Academy of Pediatrics (AAP) 2014 clinical report, "Anterior Cruciate Ligament Injuries: Diagnosis, Treatment, and Prevention," the risk for injuring the ACL increases significantly at 12 to 13 years of age in girls and at 14 to 15 years of age in boys (Figure 9-1). Teenaged female athletes are reported to have a 4- to 8-times higher risk of ACL injury than teenaged male athletes because female athletes tend to use their muscles differently than male athletes doing sports skills such as jumping and landing. The most common type of ACL injury seen in female athletes occurs by a noncontact mechanism. A noncontact ACL injury in sports is an injury in which the athlete tears the ACL during an awkward movement that does not involve direct contact with another athlete. On average, 70% to 78% of ACL injuries occur without contact, such as from a sudden twisting motion in the knee when an athlete lands or steps. During puberty, body size increases in both sexes, but boys get a burst of testosterone, which results in larger, stronger muscles. Girls do not get this rapid growth in muscle power.

Preventing an ACL Injury

The AAP has a very helpful video for preventing ACL injuries in young athletes (see the Resource section at the end of this chapter). It advises parents of adolescents at higher risk for ACL injuries because of their chosen sport (eg, basketball, volleyball, soccer) to enroll their adolescent in specific neuromuscular training programs before sports participation. This training consists of a series of exercises to strengthen the key muscles that protect the knee. Many studies demonstrate that these programs are helpful in preventing ACL injury.

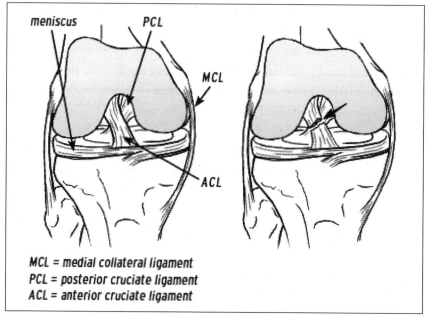

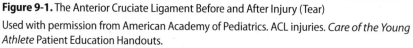

Figure 9-1. The Anterior Cruciate Ligament Before and After Injury (Tear)
Used with permission from American Academy of Pediatrics. ACL injuries. *Care of the Young Athlete* Patient Education Handouts.

What Is Concussion?

A concussion is caused by a bang, blow, or jolt to the head. Concussions also can occur from a blow to the body that results in the head moving abruptly forward and back. When the head moves abruptly this way, the brain does as well, and it can be injured. Even what seems to be a mild hit to the head can sometimes be serious. Adolescents, with their still-developing brains, are more susceptible to concussion, and any injury to the head needs to be addressed correctly. The following are key points about concussions in children and teens:

- Young children and teens are more likely to experience a concussion, and they can take longer to recover than adults.

- In 2012, a child was seen in an emergency department every 3 minutes for a sports-related concussion.

- Among high school athletes, concussion rates have risen 200% in the past decade.

- Recognizing and properly responding to a concussion when it first occurs can help prevent further injury or even death.

- Preventing injuries is critical. While healing from a concussion, children and teens are at a greater risk of sustaining another concussion. To avoid more serious injury while the brain is in this vulnerable position, athletes should avoid playing and practicing until appropriately approved by their pediatrician to resume exercise or sports.

The Signs and Symptoms of a Concussion

Concussions, when handled properly, usually get better. How can you tell if your child needs care for a head injury? Unfortunately, one can't see a concussion. Signs and symptoms of a concussion can appear immediately after an injury or may not be noticed until hours or days after the injury. You must be alert for changes in how your teen is acting or feeling. If the symptoms are getting worse, or if your teen just "doesn't feel right," you should contact your child's doctor. Interestingly, and contrary to what some people may believe, most concussions occur without loss of consciousness.

Determining Whether Your Teen Sustained a Concussion

To determine whether your teen has experienced a concussion, you can look for certain symptoms and ask about other symptoms. The following symptoms are those that parents can look for in their teen:

- Dazed or stunned appearance
- Confusion about events
- Slow answers to questions
- Questions are repeated by the teen
- No recollection of events before or after the hit, bump, or fall
- Loss of consciousness (even briefly)
- Behavior or personality changes
- Forgetting class schedule or assignments

The following symptoms are those that teens may tell you or that you can ask about:

- Difficulty thinking or remembering
- Difficulty thinking clearly
- Difficulty concentrating
- Feeling slow
- Feeling sluggish, hazy, foggy, or groggy

The following are symptoms connected with physical changes:

- Headache or "pressure" in head
- Nausea or vomiting
- Balance problems or dizziness
- Fatigue or tiredness
- Blurry or double vision
- Sensitivity to light or noise
- Numbness or tingling
- Not "feeling right"

The following are symptoms connected with emotional changes:

- Irritability
- Sadness
- Showing more emotion than usual
- Nervousness

The following are symptoms connected with sleep (to be asked only if the injury occurred on the previous day):

- Drowsiness
- Sleeping less than usual
- Sleeping more than usual
- Trouble falling asleep

If you notice that your teen has one or more of these symptoms, you should not hesitate to discuss this with your teen's pediatrician. If a concussion has occurred, you will need to know how to best handle your teen's care. Importantly, children and teens with a concussion should never return to sports or recreation activities on the same day that the injury occurred.

Follow-up and Concussion Recovery

Sometimes a concussion checklist is used during concussion recovery (Table 9-1). The teen typically fills out the checklist to give the pediatrician a baseline of his or her particular symptoms and a severity

Table 9-1. Concussion Checklist

Circle One for Each Listed	None	Mild		Moderate		Severe	
Headache	0	1	2	3	4	5	6
"Pressure in head"	0	1	2	3	4	5	6
Neck pain	0	1	2	3	4	5	6
Nausea or vomiting	0	1	2	3	4	5	6
Dizziness	0	1	2	3	4	5	6
Blurred or double vision	0	1	2	3	4	5	6
Balance problems	0	1	2	3	4	5	6
Sensitive to light	0	1	2	3	4	5	6
Sensitive to noise	0	1	2	3	4	5	6
Feeling slowed down	0	1	2	3	4	5	6
Feeling "in a fog"	0	1	2	3	4	5	6
"Don't feel right"	0	1	2	3	4	5	6
Difficulty concentrating	0	1	2	3	4	5	6
Difficulty remembering	0	1	2	3	4	5	6
Fatigue or low energy	0	1	2	3	4	5	6
Confusion	0	1	2	3	4	5	6
Drowsiness	0	1	2	3	4	5	6
Trouble falling asleep	0	1	2	3	4	5	6
More emotional	0	1	2	3	4	5	6
Irritability	0	1	2	3	4	5	6
Sadness	0	1	2	3	4	5	6
Nervous or anxious	0	1	2	3	4	5	6

rating of those symptoms. It is then possible for the pediatrician to monitor the concussion and score the checklist to see the progress of recovery. It is not necessary for the teen to have no symptoms to return to school or to begin graduated exercise.

Returning to School and Sports After Concussion

After a concussion is diagnosed, the next challenge for your teen is returning to school or sports. Your teen's pediatrician or sports medicine specialist will make recommendations based on the severity of symptoms and, often in conjunction with a school team consisting of the school nurse, sometimes the school physician, and/or educators, will advise on when returning is appropriate and in what capacity. However, you will make the ultimate decision of when your teen returns to school or athletics. Box 9-2 presents guidelines on how to make this decision properly. It is not unusual for the school curriculum to be adjusted in the early phases of a concussion recovery. Teens may need to take rest breaks, spend fewer hours at school, be given more time to take tests or complete assignments, receive help with schoolwork, and reduce time spent reading, writing, working on the computer, playing video games, or using the phone.

Your teen's pediatrician and school team can help with managing his or her care after a concussion and help your teen return to feeling well once again. For most kids, the symptoms resolve in a week to 10 days, but for some it can take several weeks and, sometimes, months. If the concussion has not improved quickly, your pediatrician may ask that a specialist such as a pediatric sports medicine specialist or pediatric neurologist be involved in your teen's care. A return to activities requires an evaluation by your teen's pediatrician or other health care professional experienced in assessing concussions. Your teen's pediatrician or specialist will tell you when it is safe for your teen to return to begin a gradual progression of exercise and sports. This means that, until permitted, your teen should sit out of physical education class, sports practices or games, and any other type of physical activity.

A teen does not have to be free of symptoms to return to play; however, the teen should not return to play before at least a 24-hour period after the injury has occurred and permission from a health care professional such as your teen's pediatrician has been obtained. When it is considered safe and appropriate for your teen to return to play, your school should have a return-to-play protocol, supervised by the school nurse, or sometimes the school physician, consisting of a stepwise return to activity. The level of activity is consistently increased, and the teen is assessed for symptoms. If there are any problems during the protocol, the progression is stopped, and activity level does not increase until the teen is free of symptoms at that level of play.

Preventing Concussions

It would be ideal if sports could be played without a risk of injury, but after accepting that this is impossible, we can avoid many concussion injuries if we take the following precautions:

- Limiting contact during sports practices (when appropriate for the sport). In particular, there should be a zero-tolerance policy for headfirst hits and other types of illegal tackles. These tackles can lead to severe head and neck injuries and are the leading cause of severe injuries in football.

- Putting in place rule changes to help reduce the chances of injury or banning or limiting the use of certain drills or techniques.

- Checking sports equipment often, including making sure the equipment fit the athletes well, is in good condition, is stored properly, and is repaired and replaced based on instructions from the equipment companies.

Sample Approach for Determining a Student's Readiness to Return to Learning Following a Concussion

If a student athlete experiences symptoms enough to affect his or her ability to concentrate or deal with stimulation such as listening, writing, or reading for 30 minutes, the student should likely remain at home. The student may consider doing light mental activities, such as watching TV, light reading, and interaction with the family, until symptoms begin. Computer use, texting, and video games should remain at a minimum. When the student athlete is able to deal with stimuli comfortably for 30 to 45 minutes, the parent may consider returning him or her back to learning, either through home tutoring or in-school instruction with programming adjustment as needed. However, it is the parent who should communicate with the school about the concussion and sign a release of information for school personnel to coordinate adjustments that may be needed as recommended by the primary care physician. The level of adjustments are decided jointly by the parent, school, and primary care physician based on severity, type, and duration of symptoms present.

Source: Reproduced with permission from Pediatrics, Vol. 132, Page 952, Copyright © 2013 by the AAP

Sports Specialization

Sports specialization is typical in youth sports for a variety of reasons. The media coverage at national and international competition in sports such as gymnastics, figure skating, swimming, diving, and tennis gives us an idea of the focus placed on many talented, yet young, competitive athletes. Some kids may seek to emulate such sports heroes and dream of a professional sports career, while others imagine winning a college scholarship. An obsession with success in competitive sports may be internally driven by the child or externally driven by the parent. The motivation may occur even though the likelihood of achieving such success in sports is very low. There may be advantages to sports specialization with teens, especially if they are looking to enter the circuit of serious competition or a professional career, but the AAP recommends avoiding specialization in a single sport before puberty. Children who specialize in a sport too early may experience physical and psychological negative effects.

Sports Considerations and the Early Bloomer

When a child begins puberty early (boys younger than 9 years and girls younger than 8 years), parents may be unaware of the particular painful experiences this might bring for their children. For children, anything that sets them apart from their peers and calls attention to something that is different about them is probably not received in a positive way.

Parents and coaches, however, may see an early blooming boy or girl as having the potential for some significant advantage in sports. The early bloomer may get picked for sports teams simply because of his or her size as compared with average-sized kids, regardless of any athletic ability! Remember that organized sports leagues tend to group kids by age instead of developmental skill. Just as it is unrealistic to expect children at the same age to all have the same academic level, it is equally unrealistic to expect children of the same age to have the same physical development, motor skills, and physical capacity. Some children will grow at lightning speed as early bloomers and others at a much slower pace as late bloomers.

Early bloomers typically will enjoy advantages in sports due to their size and strength in comparison with those growing at a slower pace. Parents and coaches can emphasize to young athletes that improvement depends on developing proper skills and not just relying on size. This can be invaluable to early bloomers who might otherwise neglect developing their skills. Eventually, the other kids will catch up in size.

Anticipating this reality of puberty, this leveling of the playing field, and encouraging the early bloomer to train accordingly can mitigate much disappointment and feelings of not measuring up or even of failure that may occur when other kids catch up in size and increase their athletic abilities. On the physical side, it is certainly important to remember that these early bloomers still have immature bones and are susceptible to injuries.

Sports Considerations and the Late Bloomer

Our society places a heavy emphasis on winning. Being a late bloomer and loving organized sports competition can be difficult because children are placed in competition against other children of similar age and not of similar ability or physical maturity.

Many talented young athletes who are late bloomers funnel out of the sports pipeline far too soon because of their temporary lack of ability, which is merely because of a delay in puberty. Many quit because they think their struggles are due to a lack of competence when really it is because of delayed physical growth. Many famous athletes, such as basketball star Michael Jordan, who, at 5'11", was originally cut from his junior varsity high school team, went on to become successful sports players after having a growth spurt. It sometimes is easy to get caught up in the competitive spirit of organized sports, but it is important not to show disappointment if your child does not become MVP. The important thing is that your child continues to play and develop, improves existing skills and learns new skills, and enjoys the athletic experience. As much as possible, I encourage parents and coaches to recognize the value in giving all players equal attention and the playing time needed to develop their skills.

The Negative Aspects of Early Sports Specialization

A child who specializes in one sport too early might encounter some negative aspects and experience a decrease in lifelong physical activity. Some of the negative aspects of specializing in a sport too early include

- Social isolation from peers who do not participate in the sport.
- Altered relationships with family because of constant, intense training.
- Overdependence on others, such as coaches.
- Delays in behavioral development or having socially unacceptable behaviors.
- Overuse injuries, burnout, anxiety, depression, and quitting. These conditions are increased in athletes who wish to specialize early.

- Lack of exposure to a variety of other sports that the young athlete might truly enjoy, excel at, or want to participate in throughout his or her adult life.

- Possible dietary and chemical manipulation.

Additionally, young athletes who train intensively, whether they are specializing or not, can also be at risk for experiencing these adverse effects. However, correctly timed sports specialization that is not started before puberty may help kids reach specific goals. As discussed earlier, physical literacy is the process used to give children younger than 12 years the tools to have the ability, confidence, and desire to be active for life. Children with athletic competence can sample many different sports, which prepares them to continue playing into the teenage years and beyond. Academic experts in the field of youth and athletic development know that encouraging early sports diversity, contrary to what many coaches and parents believe, better prepares athletes to play at the college level and beyond. Therefore, experts recommend delaying specialization in one sport until after puberty has begun. Children may have a favorite activity such as gymnastics, tennis, and hockey, but they should engage in many other activities before puberty to build overall athletic competence.

The following AAP guidance helps parents to address children and teens (younger than 18 years) who are considering specialization or have already specialized:

1. **The primary focus of sports for young athletes should be to have fun and learn lifelong physical activity skills.**
   Although it is wonderful to dream and to dream big, realistically, when it comes to athletics, most teens will not achieve Olympic greatness or have a professional sports career. At all times, for the sake of promoting lifelong health and wellness, parents are advised to first help their kids develop a love and appreciation of being physically active for life. Everyone needs to be physically literate.

2 **Participating in multiple sports, at least until puberty, decreases the chances of injuries, stress, and burnout in young athletes.**
Involvement in any sport or specializing in that sport when too young can lead to psychological burnout. More than 3.5 million children aged 14 years and younger are injured annually during sports and recreation. At least half of these injuries are from overuse. Overuse injuries in teens can be much more serious than at other ages because their growth plates can be damaged during the adolescent growth spurt.

3 **For most sports, later specialization in a sport (ie, late adolescence) may result in a young athlete's higher chance of accomplishing athletic goals.**
Research suggests that delaying sports specialization for most sports until after puberty (late adolescence, approximately 15 or 16 years of age) will minimize the risks and result in a higher likelihood of athletic success.

4 **Early diversification and delayed specialization provide a greater chance of lifetime sports involvement, lifetime physical fitness, and, possibly, elite participation.**
Playing many sports early has a greater potential of reducing dropouts while keeping kids interested in participating longer, helping create positive peer relationships and leadership skills, and creating internal motivation by participating in enjoyable activities.

5 **If your child expresses interest in specializing in a single sport, discuss goals with him or her to determine whether they are appropriate. This type of discussion may help children understand their own goals separate from those of coaches or from you.**
Studies have shown that parents were the strongest influence on starting a sport, and coaches influenced the decision to train intensely and specialize in a sport.

6. **It is important for parents to closely monitor the training and coaching environment of "elite" youth sports programs and be aware of best practices for their children's sports.**

   Many theories exist about how to achieve athletic success. A parent's strategy to guide his or her child must be centered on evidence-based and best-practice advice. For instance, it is often misinterpreted that 10,000 hours of practice or competition is needed for an athlete to succeed. This information was deduced and incorrectly applied by the media, based on studies conducted about success in chess players. There is no evidence that this theory is sensible, and additional evidence shows that many athletes succeed with fewer hours of play and many do not succeed with more hours of play.

7. **Throughout the year, taking off at least 3 months in 1-month increments from a particular sport of interest will allow for your child's physical and psychological recovery.**

   Young athletes may still remain active in other sports during this time off from their sport of interest to maintain fitness levels, strength, flexibility, and skill development.

8. **Young athletes who take off at least 1 to 2 days per week from their particular sport of interest can decrease the risk of overuse injuries.**

   It is important to safeguard against overuse injuries. Having time off is one way to avoid sustaining overuse injuries.

9. **Closely monitoring physical and psychological growth, maturation, and a healthy diet in young athletes who train intensively is important.**

   Parents may not be aware of how intensive training affects their teen's calorie needs at the same time their body has special requirements for ongoing growth. Good caloric intake of healthy foods is necessary to provide fuel for exercise and growth. Athletes must eat foods rich in iron, the proper amount of calcium, and vitamin D. Iron plays a role in supporting oxygen transport, aerobic muscle metabolism, and proper cognition, while calcium and vitamin D are needed to support healthy bone growth. When considering proper growth, in certain sports, such as gymnastics, figure skating, long-distance running, or dance, it is considered optimal to have a very slim physique. The possibility of disordered eating behaviors, such as anorexia nervosa or bulimia, may be increased in these situations. Parents should be on the lookout for the *female triad,* which refers to the combination of 3 conditions that affects some female athletes. The three conditions are low energy (with or without an eating disorder), lack of menstruation (or menstrual irregularity), and low bone density. Usually the teenaged girl is not eating enough to meet her training and growth demands. Stress fractures can be a sign of low bone density.

The Value of Physical Fitness

Physical literacy is a crucial element for the success of children's and teens' overall health and wellness. Athletics and sports have an integral role in keeping adolescents' bodies physically fit—but also in optimal brain development. By understanding the connection between physical activity and a child's or teen's total health and well-being, parents can proactively take a bigger role in advocating for physical literacy. Children who are physically competent to play sports before age 12 years have the opportunity to reap the physical, emotional, and cognitive benefits of sports. Further, as advocates for children, parents can make it possible for children of all abilities and those with disabilities to enjoy the same benefits. Parents who are armed with evidence-based knowledge about how best to guide their kids in competitive sports can better plan strategies for their children's success. If you and your child's goal is to become an Olympic athlete, the best road to success is not to consider specializing in sports until puberty. Parents who understand the interaction of puberty with sports know best how to safeguard their child to have a positive experience and continue to play sports through puberty and longer.

Resource

American Academy of Pediatrics. Preventing ACL injuries in young athletes. HealthyChildren.org Web site. **https://www.healthychildren.org/ English/health-issues/injuries-emergencies/sports-injuries/Pages/ Preventing-ACL-Injuries-in-Young-Athletes-Video.aspx**. Updated November 21, 2015. Accessed May 8, 2018

CHAPTER 10

Caring About Health and Wellness

You may often despair over your teen's food choices, sleep habits, or significant lack of physical activity, and you may have tried discussing these concerns with your teen but feel you did not get through to him or her. Though you might not be able to see it, your teenager is invested in what you say, even though he or she seems totally oblivious to everything.

Most adolescents care very much about wellness, but they don't want to admit it in front of their parents. Often, they act ambivalent about healthy habits in front of their family, but privately they admit that wellness matters greatly to them. However, they often lack the will-power to eat properly, sustain regular activity, keep healthy sleep habits, or hydrate adequately.

Change is one of the most difficult things to accomplish, and the best advice to teens is to have them choose something that they can change without turning their lives inside out. Even a few small improvements they are confident they can stick with are rewarding. Small changes can make a big difference. Further, success in a small change gives teens confidence and momentum to make more change.

Health Hygiene—The Elements of Wellness

The elements of wellness are known as health hygiene. Caring about health hygiene goes a long way toward a successful *health destiny*. The 4 components of good health hygiene are water hygiene, activity hygiene, sleep hygiene, and dietary hygiene.

Hydration is key to how we feel and perform, yet water hygiene, or daily water intake, often is ignored. Many basic health issues can be addressed with proper hydration, and many issues that teens regularly complain about, such as headaches, fatigue, and poor athletic performance, often have their roots in simple water intake that is not being well managed.

Activity hygiene is a teen's structured daily activity, or exercise. More specifically, it is the extent to which a teen is getting the daily recommended amount of physical activity.

Sleep hygiene pertains to sleep patterns. We understand more today than ever before about the specific nuances concerning adolescent sleep and the importance of good sleep quality and quantity.

Dietary hygiene pertains to the teen's everyday dietary patterns and how balancing various nutritional components contributes to total health and wellness.

Water Hygiene

Approximately 60% of our body mass consists of water, and dehydration can directly affect the proper functioning of all organ systems and contribute to many health issues. Daily water requirements may vary somewhat, but, generally, a teen should drink between 6 and 8 cups a day, along with the recommended servings of fruits and vegetables, which supply hydration as well. These requirements change with activity level, and if the teen is active, the amount of water needed also increases. Hydration before, during, and after exercise is important. Exercising outside in hot weather affects hydration as well. During exercise, and depending on the level of exertion, a teen should drink between

½ cup (4 oz) and 2 cups (16 oz) of water every 15 to 20 minutes. If exercise continues for longer than 1 hour, having a sports drink is acceptable because it appropriately replaces any lost electrolytes and carbohydrates, which is not necessary with shorter workouts.

The overall use of caffeine by teenagers has not changed much in recent years, but the different sources by which they get the caffeine has. Teens are less likely today to be drinking large amounts of caffeinated soda but do consume a lot of energy drinks and coffee. Caffeine has diuretic properties, which means it can increase water loss from the body and increase the risk of dehydration in adolescents. These products should be avoided in order to maintain good hydration.

Activity Hygiene

Children and adolescents need to engage in 1 hour or more of daily physical activity. Most of this time should include moderate-intensity aerobic activity; however, at least 3 of the days each week should include some vigorous-intensity physical activity as well. In addition, on at least 3 of the days of the week, some exercise should focus on muscle strengthening, and on at least another 3 days each week, bone-strengthening activities should be included. Table 10-1 offers various types of activities that serve as a guide. Encourage your child or adolescent to try each activity if age-appropriate.

Whatever the physical activity chosen, it should be age appropriate, fun, and enjoyable, and have enough variety to keep adolescents interested. One of the most critical obstacles to regular activity is that kids might not enjoy what they are doing. Make the experience fun, and they will be excited to participate, such as setting up scavenger hunts outside to get the whole family moving, going to the gym together for a game of basketball, or signing up for a dance or cycling class.

Table 10-1. Types of Aerobic and Muscle- and Bone-Strengthening Activities

Type of Physical Activity	Age Group	
	Children	Adolescents
Moderate-intensity aerobic	Active recreation such as hiking, skateboarding, rollerblading Bicycle riding Walking to school	Active recreation, such as canoeing, hiking, cross-country skiing, skateboarding, rollerblading Brisk walking Bicycle riding House and yard work such as sweeping Playing games that require catching and throwing, such as baseball, softball, basketball, and volleyball
Vigorous-intensity aerobic	Active games involving running and chasing, such as tag Bicycle riding Jumping rope Martial arts, such as karate Running Sports such as ice or field hockey, basketball, swimming, tennis, or gymnastics	Active games involving running and chasing, such as flag football, soccer Bicycle riding Jumping rope Martial arts such as karate Running Sports such as tennis, ice or field hockey, basketball, swimming Vigorous dancing Aerobics Cheerleading or gymnastics
Muscle-strengthening	Games such as tug of war Modified push-ups (with knees on the floor) Resistance exercises using body weight or resistance bands Sit-ups Swinging on playground equipment/bars Gymnastics	Games such as tug of war Push-ups Resistance exercises with exercise bands, weight machines, hand-held weights Rock climbing Sit-ups Cheerleading or gymnastics
Bone-strengthening	Games such as hop-scotch Hopping, skipping, jumping Jumping rope Running Sports such as gymnastics, basketball, volleyball, tennis	Hopping, skipping, jumping Jumping rope Running Sports such as gymnastics, basketball, volleyball, tennis

Adapted from https://www.cdc.gov/physicalactivity/basics/children/what_counts.htm

Differentiating Between Moderate and Vigorous Activity

Often, a motivated teen would like to start doing some physical activity but doesn't know what type of activity is moderate or vigorous. The chart from ChooseMyPlate.gov (Table 10-2) can be very useful for a teen who is interested in knowing about the types of activities he or she might consider doing as well as the level of activity that would be satisfied by doing this activity for either 30 minutes or 1 hour. In addition, the chart notes the number of calories the teen can expect to burn during that period.

The calories spent for each activity listed in Table 10-2 are based on a 154-pound male who is 5'10" tall. Those individuals who weigh more will use more calories; those who weigh less will use fewer calories. The calorie values listed include the calories used by the activity and those used for normal body functioning during the activity time.

Table 10-2. Moderate and Vigorous Activities and Calories Burned

MODERATE Physical Activities	Calories Burned in 1 h	Calories Burned in 30 min
Hiking	370	185
Light gardening/yard work	330	165
Dancing	330	165
Golf (walking and carrying clubs)	330	165
Bicycling (slower than 10 mph)	290	145
Walking (3.5 mph)	280	140
Weight training (general light workout)	220	110
Stretching	180	90
VIGOROUS Physical Activities	**Calories Burned in 1 h**	**Calories Burned in 30 min**
Running/jogging (5 mph)	590	295
Bicycling (faster than 10 mph)	590	295
Swimming (slow freestyle laps)	510	255
Aerobics	480	240
Walking (4.5 mph)	460	230
Heavy yard work (chopping wood)	440	220
Weight lifting (vigorous effort)	440	220
Basketball (vigorous)	440	220

Adapted from www.choosemyplate.gov/physical-activity-calories-burn

Barriers to Appropriate Activity Hygiene

Many factors can hinder a teen's activity hygiene. Parents can help monitor these and how they affect their teen.

Screen Time

No contemporary discussion of improving activity hygiene is possible without emphasizing the importance of limiting screen time. Among the distinct barriers to adolescents getting the recommended daily amount of physical activity is their increased sedentary behaviors, particularly watching TV. Excessive television screen time is a factor in children and teens having overweight and obesity. The association of TV watching and weight issues in teens is surprisingly independent of the amount of physical activity an adolescent might get.

Media and the Food and Beverage Industry

For years, the food and beverage industry has used to their own advantage the knowledge that children and teens spend hours in front of the TV. Through various marketing and advertising techniques, the food and beverage industry encourages the development of unhealthy food preferences in children of all ages. Children are exposed to countless ads on TV and streaming services and through video games, social media, and most Internet Web sites. This is one of many important reasons why the American Academy of Pediatrics (AAP) recommends that, except for video chatting with loved ones, screen time should be avoided from birth to 18 months of age.

> **American Academy of Pediatrics Screen Time Guidelines**
>
> The American Academy of Pediatrics screen time guidelines also emphasize the role that media can play in disrupting healthy eating habits, such as when media is on during family mealtimes. Families can set important limits with screen time by creating a family media plan that includes screen-free zones, such as at the dinner table. You can access information at HealthyChildren.org (https://www.healthychildren.org/MediaUsePlan) for more information on exactly how to do this.

A Lack of Athletic Confidence

Not every person has natural athletic ability and probably even more people are unaware of their potential ability. Lacking confidence in athletic ability by puberty is an enormous barrier to being or becoming active. If your teen lacks self confidence in this area, talk with your teen and suggest signing him or her up for classes that your teen will enjoy, such as dance, swimming, tennis, or yoga. Your local library or online video streaming subscription may also have exercise programs for your teen to do at home. For many teens the biggest fear may be starting or joining an activity. Once they become more familiar and comfortable with the activity, they might become more willing to join other activities.

Starting an Activity Program

Many teens wish to start an activity program. Some of them believe that a gym membership or owning expensive equipment is necessary. Neither a gym membership nor expensive equipment is necessary. Exercise is a wonderful medicine, and everyone is able to start on the road to health and wellness without breaking the bank. Simple ways to get moving can include walks with your family outside, joining a community league such as basketball or volleyball, signing up for the local walk or 5k, pushups, leg or chair squats, and lunges. Tables 10-1 and 10-2 also provide various activities that can be fun while getting your teen active.

I am proud to be a USA Level 1 Adult and Youth and Junior triathlon coach. A triathlon is a race with 3 separate parts: swimming, biking, and running. It is an awesome sport for anyone, but it has certain unique characteristics that make it a great choice for the teen who doesn't feel confident about athletics or doesn't love team sports. Triathlon distances tend to increase with the participant's age. While all the distances have merit, the sprint distance is an attainable and healthy training distance for children and teens. There are many reasons short distance triathlon training and racing is worth suggesting you do together as a family. If you are interested, please read my article, "Sprint Distance Triathlon: A Lifetime Sport for All Ages," at **https://www.healthychildren.org/English/healthy-living/sports/Pages/Sprint-Distance-Triathlon-A-Lifetime-Sport.aspx**

The following are the different types of races:

Sprint: Sprint triathlon distances vary from venue to venue. A typical sprint race would consist of a 500-m to 750-m swim, a 20-km bike race, and a 5-km run.

Olympic: The Olympic race is the distance that is used in the Olympics—a 1.5-km swim, a 40-km bike race, and a 10-km run.

Half Ironman: The total distance of a half Ironman is 70.3 miles and consists of a 1.9-km swim, a 90-km bike race, and a 21.1-km run.

Ironman: The Ironman is the biggest triathlon with a total of 140.6 miles. It consists of a 3.8-km swim, a 180-km bike race, and a 42.2-km run.

Sleep Hygiene

The National Institutes of Health estimates that teenagers need at least 9 hours of sleep per night; however, only 9% of high school students actually meet these recommendations. Even more alarming is the fact that 20% are getting by on fewer than 5 hours of sleep per night. Contrary to popular parental belief, teens need more sleep, not less, than they did in previous years. Teens from ages 13 to 18 years require 8 to 10 hours of sleep, including naps, in a 24-hour period. Chronic lack of proper sleep can directly affect a teen's ability to be at his or her best at school, in sports or activities, or with friends or family. Some of the consequences of lack of proper sleep in adolescents have been associated with the following:

- Cognitive difficulties, especially with more complex tasks

- Increased risk of high blood pressure and stroke

- Weight gain

- Depression, anxiety, irritability, and suicidal ideation

- Poor school attendance

- Difficulties with memory

- Increase in motor vehicle crashes

- Less physical activity

The Biology of Sleep During Puberty

At approximately the beginning of puberty, a sleep-wake "phase delay" takes place and results in a change in your child's body of the time at which he or she gets sleepy. Your child will start to fall asleep later and will want and need to wake up later. The shift in bedtime can be as much as 2 hours compared with what it had previously been in middle childhood. This interesting phenomenon is believed to be caused by 2 principal biological changes that occur in sleep regulation.

The first is a change in when melatonin is released. Melatonin is a hormone that is released by a tiny gland in the brain and plays an important role in causing sleepiness. In teens, melatonin is released later and results in a shift in when feeling tired occurs, making it difficult to impossible to be able to fall asleep at the previous earlier bedtime. This change is occurring at the same time as a change in the body's natural circadian rhythms. Circadian rhythm is best described as the body's internal biological clock. It controls the timing of many of the biological processes that take place in our daily bodily functions. The normal human pattern of circadian rhythm waxes and wanes in a distinct pattern throughout the 24-hour day. In adolescence, this up-and-down cycling of sleep and wakefulness shifts, referred to as a shift in "circadian phase" alongside the changes in melatonin. As a result, most teens cannot fall asleep before 11:00 pm and their optimal time to wake up is around 8:00 am.

The other biological change is an adjustment in adolescents' "sleep drive." Adolescents' need to fall asleep develops more slowly, and they no longer have the same urgency to get to sleep that they used to have. Because of these changes, your teen simply finds it a lot easier and usually more desirable to stay up later. In the past, prevailing thought was that teens just wanted to stay up late and their reluctance to go to sleep earlier, even though it was clearly the responsible choice, represented yet another example of the rebellious and immature behaviors that are the hallmark of adolescence. We now know that this has much less to do with rebellion and much more to do with sleep physiology.

The biological factors affecting adolescents' sleep have some important ramifications for well-being through puberty. Most teens, on average, have a bedtime 2 hours later than they did before the onset of puberty, but they will continue to wake up at the same time as they previously did or even earlier if required for school attendance. The delay that they have in getting to sleep becomes an issue when they miss out on REM episodes in the morning hours; REM is the deepest level of sleep needed to recharge teens' batteries. Parents should be expecting their teen to get 8 to 10 hours of sleep a night, with the optimal range between 8½ and 9½ hours per night. Teens get fewer than 7 hours of sleep nightly but still need the same amount, or possibly more, than they did before puberty. Social factors such as phone calls, Internet browsing, video games, or texting can also affect how much quality sleep your teen receives. Parents should monitor how much television or computer time their teen engages in daily, making sure that their teen is screen free for at least 1 hour prior to bed and ensuring that no TVs, computers, or phones are kept in their teen's bedroom.

A poll taken by the National Sleep Foundation found that 71% of parents believed that their adolescent was getting a sufficient amount of sleep. This mismatch indicates a significant lack of awareness among parents of the extent of adolescent sleep loss. Bringing parental awareness to this significant health issue will hopefully encourage a discussion of how best to resolve this. When your teen doesn't receive adequate sleep, there can be huge health and safety consequences.

Consequences of Adolescent Sleep Deprivation

- **Low grades and poor school performance.** Teens are chronically sleep deprived. Throughout the school week they awaken early and start their academic day with an energy deficit, often feeling unrested and struggling to learn. Insufficient sleep has an effect on academic performance and affects attention, memory, behavior control, and cognition. In the National Sleep Foundation poll, 28% of students reported falling asleep in school at least once a week, and more than 1 in 5 fell asleep doing homework with similar frequency. High school students who admit to having academic problems, generally earning Cs, Ds, or failing grades, get less sleep, have later bedtimes, and have more irregular sleep schedules than those students who get enough sleep and report higher grades. This type of occurrence has been demonstrated at the middle school, high school, and college levels. Lack of sleep is also associated with higher rates of absenteeism, chronic lateness, and decreased readiness to learn.

- **Physical injury and safety risks.** The risk of unintentional injuries and death is increased by lack of proper sleep. Drowsiness or fatigue has been identified as a principal cause in at least 100,000 traffic crashes each year. Sleep loss and fatigue pose a significant increase in the chances of these accidents occurring.

- **Anxiety and mood disorders.** An increase in anxiety disorders, as well as an increase in suicidal ideation (mood disorders such as depression and suicidal thoughts) are linked to poor quality of and insufficient sleep in adolescents. Suicide is the second leading cause of preventable death in adolescents, so appropriate sleep is an important factor when thinking about suicide prevention.

- **Increased use of unsafe products.** To combat the effects of insufficient sleep, some teens use stimulants and prescription products, as well as smoke cigarettes and use related nicotine products.

- **Metabolic dysfunction.** Poor sleep habits have been shown to affect blood glucose metabolism, possibly resulting in type 2 diabetes and problems regulating cholesterol, which may contribute to heart disease.

- **Obesity.** Several studies have shown that short sleep time is associated with obesity in children and adolescents. It might be because lack of sleep disrupts the appropriate levels of insulin and leads to poor blood glucose control. Further, a hormone called ghrelin, which promotes hunger, has been shown to be increased with lack of sleep. A hormone called leptin, which regulates the feeling of fullness, also does not have normal levels in people whose sleep time is too short. This may explain the "midnight munchies" that so many teens experience while up late, especially those in college.

Advocating for Change

The typical high school start time is not optimal given teens' sleep needs. Typically, teens go to sleep too late all week long and then try to catch up on the weekends. We refer to this as "social jet lag." Most people are familiar with jet lag, which describes the way a person feels after flying across time zones. The time that it gets dark and when it becomes light has changed, but the person's circadian rhythm, or biological clock, has not. This makes it difficult to fall asleep at the new bedtime. It also is common to not feel entirely well or adjusted until the biological clock resets. It takes about 1 day for every hour of time change for people to feel well once their biological clock has been interrupted.

The teen's effort to catch up on lost sleep never works out well because, although it may solve some of the problems from lack of sleep, it often disturbs the circadian rhythms and results in morning sleepiness at school.

The AAP recognizes that this regular lack of proper sleep by most adolescents should be considered a public health issue because the consequences are affecting the health, safety, and academic success of middle and high school students across the United States. The AAP has been advocating for middle and high schools to delay the start of classes until 8:30 am or later to accommodate the sleep-wake cycles of adolescents. Making the adjustment to later school start times, no earlier than 8:30 am, has been estimated to have the potential of adding roughly $9 billion a year to the US economy, which would come primarily from 2 sources: greater academic performance (and hence, lifetime earnings) among more well-rested students, and reduced rates of car crashes among sleepy teen drivers. The later start time would allow teens to get the sleep that they need to be successful and also help as a safety measure. Parents can and need to work together with local school boards to advocate for this to become policy.

Encouraging Proper Sleep

- **Keep an eye on screen time.** Another newly recognized problem regarding proper sleep is called digital toxicity, which refers to the light emitted from electronic devices. This light has been shown to decrease the production of melatonin, a necessary ingredient for proper sleep. The AAP recommends that all screens—TVs, computers, laptops, tablets, and cell phones—be kept out of your teen's bedroom, especially at night.

- **Make the bedroom dark and peaceful.** If too much light can get in, consider adding dark drapes or curtains and installing blinds to help darken the room at night.

- **Reduce bedroom temperature.** Contrary to what some people believe, cooler temperatures make it healthier and easier to get a good night's sleep.

- **Encourage being outdoors and active during the day.** Spending time outdoors improves circadian rhythms, and regular physical activity helps with overall health and well-being. Physical activity can cause tiredness as well and, if done earlier during the day as opposed to early evening or close to bedtime, may give your body a chance to regulate before sleep.

- **Encourage sleep as one of your family priorities.** You should model the behavior that you are looking for. If your teen sees that the family takes sleep seriously, he or she will learn to do the same. If you make exceptions to this or bend the rules to accommodate schoolwork that should have been completed earlier, your teen will develop that type of attitude in his or her own routines.

- **Encourage consistency for teens' daily schedule.** The days of trying to get your newborn to sleep through the night may be behind you, but much the same way that consistency helps a newborn get used to a bedtime routine, this remains true today with your teen. It still pays to be consistent with your schedules. Encourage your teen to get to bed at relatively the same time each night, wake up at relatively the same time, eat meals regularly, and get regular physical activity, and he or she should have more success with proper sleep. In addition, your teen needs to try to keep his or her schedule under control. It is very typical for families to have a daily routine that leaves little or no downtime. Relaxing is an important part of being able to settle down and get to sleep.

Understanding and Improving Dietary Hygiene

Good dietary hygiene depends on satisfying the daily nutrients the body needs. The ChooseMyPlate.gov Web site has free resources to track activities, food intake, and calories. Other apps available for downloading to your phone or tablet can help provide the nutritional value of many foods so that you or your teen can make an informed choice.

Diet Versus Fad

Once my teenaged patient and I have established that he or she is interested in improving dietary hygiene, we need to identify the problem areas. I explain that good health is about having a healthy lifestyle that the teen is dedicated to all the time. It is neither a "diet" nor a "fad," but it is a way of life that the teen must make into a habit.

The first thing I ask the teen is whether there is anything in his or her current lifestyle that could be changed for good. I tell the teen that he or she is allowed to cheat but needs to be honest about it and do it infrequently. I say that if the teen feels there is nothing he or she can change for good, could he or she change something a little?

Making small changes is very attainable for many teens, and many want to try. Replacing sugar-sweetened beverages with water is a very popular choice. A lot of teens feel this is something they can do most of the time. It is important that I remind them often that success is measured in very small steps; change is not something that will be obvious day to day, but when we look back over a year or more, we can see great improvements.

It doesn't really make sense to tell a teenager to eat a balanced and healthy diet if the teen has no idea what that means. Many teens admit that they believe they eat too much during the day, but they aren't really sure. To start a teen on the path to eating a healthy diet, he or she needs to learn about approximate calorie requirements.

How many calories should an adolescent be eating in a day? It depends on the adolescent's activity level. If your teen is considered sedentary because he or she does not engage in any regular activity outside of the typical day-to-day actions, the calorie requirements per day are relatively different than for an active adolescent. For instance, a 16-year-old girl who is moderately active, meaning that she engages in the equivalent of walking 1.5 to 3 miles per day at a pace of 3 to 4 miles per hour, would require approximately 2,000 calories per day; however, a 16-year-old girl who is sedentary would require approximately 1,800 calories per day. For more details on estimated daily calorie needs for adolescents at different activity levels, see Table 10-3.

Table 10-3. How Many Calories Does a Teen Need to Be Healthy?

Estimated Calorie Requirements (in kcal) for Each Gender and Age Group at 3 Levels of Physical Activity				
Gender	Age (y)	Sedentary[a]	Moderately Active[b]	Active[c]
Female	9–13	1,600	1,600–2,000	1,800–2,200
	14–18	1,800	2,000	2,400
	19–30	2,000	2,000–2,200	2,400
Male	9–13	1,800	1,800–2,200	2,000–2,600
	14–18	2,200	2,400–2,800	2,800–3,200
	19–30	2,400	2,600–2,800	3,000

[a] Sedentary means a lifestyle that includes only the light physical activity associated with typical day-to-day life.
[b] Moderately active means a lifestyle that includes physical activity equivalent to walking 1.5 to 3 miles per day at 3 to 4 miles per hour, in addition to the light physical activity associated with typical day-to-day life.
[c] Active means a lifestyle that includes physical activity equivalent to walking more than 3 miles per day at 3 to 4 miles per hour, in addition to the light physical activity associated with typical day-to-day life.

Source: Reproduced with permission from Bright Futures: Nutrition, page 102.
https://brightfutures.aap.org/Bright%20Futures%20Documents/BFNutrition3rdEditionSupervision.pdf

Ways to Achieve a Healthy Food Lifestyle

- **Eat regularly as a family.** Research has indicated that there is a relationship between having regular family meals and the quality of food choices adolescents make. The increased frequency of family meals is associated with greater intake of fruits, vegetables, and milk and with a simultaneous decrease in fried foods and carbonated beverages. The children in families that eat 5 or more meals together per week are approximately 25% less likely to encounter nutritional health issues than children who eat fewer than 1 meal per week with their families. Shared family meals seem to operate as a protective factor for having overweight, unhealthy eating, and disordered eating.

- **Serve appropriate portion sizes.** Portion size is one of the most important factors for how much a child or teen eats. When we repeatedly eat portion sizes that are too large for our energy needs, we tend to simply overeat rather than leave what we don't need on our plates. As parents, becoming educated on appropriate portion sizes and trying to stick to that amount as regularly as possible is valuable for the whole family. The ChooseMyPlate.gov Web site has great information on portion size and other issues regarding eating healthy. To help teach your family appropriate portion size and prevent overeating, dole out healthy single servings of food away from the table and don't leave bowls of food on the table. This helps everyone recognize reasonable amounts of food and reinforces this on a continuous basis. Also, when the food is not within easy reach, it makes it harder to grab for seconds.

- **Manage leftovers.** When you make food in large quantities or have a large amount of leftovers, separate the food into serving size packaging before refrigerating or freezing it. In this way, when your teen reaches in to serve himself or herself, a proper portion will automatically be available, which is great for making sure your teen eats well and has a reasonable healthy amount of food.

- **Figure out fullness cues.** So much of our eating behavior is influenced mentally. We often fail to take cues from our body that we have eaten enough. Rather, we allow the visual cues from the appearance of food on our plate to be the dominant factor for fullness. This is a long-standing habit. One way to transition to smaller portions is to put food on smaller plates, making more appropriate portions look larger; this literally tricks our brains into feeling satisfied. Eating slowly and chewing well can also help with fullness cues and portion control.

- **Model the way.** Anything that we truly want our children to understand, respect, and do, we had better be doing ourselves. When it comes to making food choices, don't expect that your child or teen will eat veggies if you don't. Every time you reach for more pasta, mashed potatoes, or rice, you can expect your child or teen to do the same.

- **Keep offering healthy foods.** You've made an awesome vegetable dish, and your teen makes an awful face at it. Or you have decided it is time to have more fresh fruit in the house, but it goes unnoticed. Should you give up? Most definitely not! It has been shown that kids may require exposure to a particular food 10 to 15 times before giving it a try in earnest. With patience, repeated exposure, and not too much nagging, you might be very surprised at the outcome.

- **Beware of restaurant serving sizes.** Restaurant portions are often enormous! Meals served in restaurants, especially fast-food places, can be more than 3 times the recommended serving size. Try eating half and bringing the rest home, or consider splitting the meal. Sometimes, choosing an appetizer as a main course will work. Even if you need to pay extra to split the serving, the benefit to your health is worth it. Most importantly, at all costs, avoid supersizing your food, such as when you buy popcorn at the movie theater. It's not a bargain when you consider the damage to your health from grossly overeating.

- **Forget about cleaning your plate.** Whatever good intentions were associated with this rule, they have outlived their usefulness. As a society, we demonstrate little ability to self-regulate our eating by recognizing our fullness. We grossly overeat, have a distorted perception of normal portions, and emotionally value food in a destructive manner. Teaching your child or teen to clean his or her plate, as opposed to recognizing how it feels to be satisfied, is a contributor to difficulties with healthy weight management. If you are still hanging on to this old-fashioned practice, let it go.

- **Junk food management.** Proactively gut the house of unhealthy junk foods. It is easier to avoid junk food if it is not at your fingertips!

Patience for Positive Change

Impatience is the single biggest obstacle to success. Most people lack the patience to try something new and to give it the time that is needed to recognize positive change. Although it is happening, change is never apparent in an instant. Many changes arise from establishing healthy habits that are not revealed on the surface. You need to have the conviction and faith that you know you are doing the right things.

As you have read throughout this book, puberty is a time when one foot is positioned for adulthood and the other is still stuck in childhood. Parents cannot expect their teens to figure out how to keep themselves healthy and well on their own. Adolescents understand and want to make all kinds of health and wellness adjustments, but they can't do it in a vacuum. They need you, their parents, to help and to model these healthy habits. It needs to become a lifestyle. Stay patient.

Have patience and live in the moment because you will want to remember all the days of your child's journey in life—yes, even these challenging days of adolescence are part of the beautiful journey.

I very much hope that aspects of this book have brightened your outlook on the magical period of parenting through puberty, even with its mood swings, acne, and growing pains!

Resources

Academy of Nutrition and Dietetics. Eat right. **https://eatright.org**. Accessed May 8, 2018
A resource that provides healthy snack and meal ideas, smart shopping tips, and information regarding nutrition and fitness.

Kowal-Connelly S. How children develop unhealthy food preferences. American Academy of Pediatrics HealthyChildren.org Web site. **https://www.healthychildren.org/English/healthy-living/nutrition/ Pages/How-Children-Develop-Unhealthy-Food-Preferences.aspx**. Updated February 25, 2017. Accessed May 8, 2018
An article about media and food advertising's effect on children that includes ideas on how parents can advocate for change.

INDEX

Page numbers followed by an *f* or a *t* denote a figure or a table, respectively.